William Bentley

A Collection of Psalms and hymns for publick worship

William Bentley

A Collection of Psalms and hymns for publick worship

ISBN/EAN: 9783337101978

Printed in Europe, USA, Canada, Australia, Japan

Cover: Foto ©Lupo / pixelio.de

More available books at **www.hansebooks.com**

SALEM:
PRINTED BY DABNEY AND CUSHING.

¶ PSALMS selected from the Psalms of DAVID, according to TATE and BRADY's Version.

PSALMS of PRAISE and ADORATION.

FIRST METRE.

PSALM I.

From the 8th of David.

1 O THOU, to whom all creatures bow
  Within this earthly frame,
Thro' all the world how great art thou,
  How glorious is thy name!

2 In heav'n thy wond'rous acts are sung,
  Nor fully reckon'd there;
And yet thou mak'st the infant tongue
  Thy boundless praise declare.

3 When heav'n, thy beaut'ous work on high,
  Employs my wond'ring sight;
The moon, that nightly rules the sky,
  With stars of feebler light;

4 What's man (say I) that, Lord, thou lov'st
  To keep him in thy mind?
Or what his offspring, that thou prov'st
  To them so wond'rous kind?

5 Him next in pow'r thou didst create
  To thy celestial train;
Ordain'd, with dignity and state,
  O'er all thy works to reign.

6 They jointly own his powerful sway;
  The beasts that prey or graze;
The bird that wings his airy way;
  The fish that cuts the seas.

7 O thou, to whom all creatures bow
  Within this earthly frame,
Thro' all the world how great art thou,
  How glorious is thy name!

PSALM II.
From the 9th of David.

1 TO celebrate thy praise, O Lord!
   I will my heart prepare,
 To all the list'ning world thy works,
   Thy wond'rous works declare.

2 The thought of them shall to my soul
   Exalted pleasures bring;
 Whilst to thy name, O thou most High,
   Triumphant praise I sing.

3 The Lord forever lives, who has
   His righteous throne prepar'd,
 Impartial justice to dispense,
   To punish or reward.

4 God is a constant, sure defence
   Against oppressing rage:
 As troubles rise, his needful aids
   In our behalf engage.

5 All those who have his goodness prov'd,
   Will in his truth confide;
 Whose mercy ne'er forsook the man
   That on his help rely'd.

PSALM

PSALM III.

From the 19th of David.

1 THE heav'ns declare thy glory, Lord,
    Which that alone can fill;
The firmament and stars express
    Their great Creator's skill.

2 The dawn of each returning day
    Fresh beams of knowledge brings;
From darkest night's successive rounds
    Divine instruction springs.

3 Their pow'rful language to no realm
    Or region is confin'd;
'Tis nature's voice, and understood
    Alike by all mankind.

4 Their doctrine does it's sacred sense
    Thro' earth's extent display;
Whose bright contents the circling sun
    Does round the world convey.

5 From east to west, from west to east,
    His restless course he goes;
And thro' his progress cheerful light
    And vital warmth bestows.

PSALM IV.

From the 33d of David.

LET all the just, to God, with joy,
    Their cheerful voices raise:
For well the righteous it becomes,
    To sing glad songs of praise.

2 For faithful is the word of God;
  His works with truth abound;
He justice loves; and all the earth
  Is with his goodness crown'd.

3 By his almighty word, at first,
  Heaven's glorious arch was rear'd;
And all the beaut'ous hosts of light
  At his command appear'd.

4 The swelling floods, together roll'd,
  He makes in heaps to lie;
And lays, as in a storehouse, safe,
  The wat'ry treasures by.

5 Let earth, and all that dwell therein,
  Before him, trembling, stand;
For, when he spake the word, 'twas made;
  'Twas fix'd at his command.

6 Whate'er the mighty Lord decrees,
  Shall stand forever sure;
The settled purpose of his heart
  To ages shall endure.

SECOND METRE.

PSALM V.

The 93d of David.

1 WITH glory clad, with strength array'd,
    The Lord, that o'er all nature reigns,
  The world's foundations strongly laid,
    And the vast fabrick still sustains.

2 How surely stablish'd is thy throne!
 Which will no change or period see;
For thou, O Lord, and thou alone,
 Art God from all eternity.

3 The floods, O Lord, lift up their voice,
 And toss the troubled waves on high;
But God above can still their noise,
 And make the angry sea comply.

4 Thy promise, Lord, is ever sure;
 And they that in thy house would dwell,
That happy station to secure,
 Must still in holiness excel.

PSALM VI.
From the 95th of David.

1 O Come, loud anthems let us sing;
 Loud thanks, to our Almighty King:
For we our voices high should raise,
When our salvation's Rock we praise.

2 Into his presence let us haste,
To thank him for his favours past:
To him address, in joyful songs,
The praise that to his name belongs.

3 For God, the Lord, enthron'd in state,
Is, with unrival'd glory, great;
A King, superiour, far, to all,
Whom by his title, God, we call.

4 The depths of earth are in his hand,
Her secret wealth at his command;
The strength of hills, that threat the skies,
Subjected to his empire lies.

5 The rolling ocean's vaſt abyſs,
   By the ſame ſov'reign right, is his;
   'Tis mov'd by his almighty hand,
   Who form'd and fix'd the ſolid land.

6 O let us to his courts repair,
   And bow with adoration there;
   Down on our knees, devoutly, all,
   Before the Lord, our maker, fall.

PSALM VII.

The 100th of David.

1 WITH one conſent, let all the earth
      To God their cheerful voices raiſe;
   Glad homage pay, with awful mirth,
      And ſing before him ſongs of praiſe.

2 Convinc'd that he is God alone,
      From whom both we and all proceed;
   We, whom he chooſes for his own,
      The flock which he vouchſafes to feed.

3 O enter then his temple gate,
      Thence to his courts devoutly preſs;
   And ſtill your grateful hymns repeat,
      And ſtill his name with praiſes bleſs.

4 For he's the Lord, ſupremely good;
      His mercy is forever ſure;
   His truth, which all times firmly ſtood,
      To endleſs ages ſhall endure.

PSALM VIII.

From the 104th of David.

1 BLESS God, my soul! Thou, Lord, alone,
    Possessest empire without bounds;
With honour thou art crown'd; thy throne
    Eternal majesty surrounds.

2 With light thou dost thyself enrobe,
    And glory for a garment take;
Heav'n's curtains stretch beyond the globe,
    Thy canopy of state to make.

3 God builds on liquid air, and forms
    His palace chambers in the skies;
The clouds his chariots are, and storms
    The swift-wing'd steeds with which he flies.

4 As bright as flame, as swift as wind,
    His ministers heav'n's palace fill,
To have their sundry tasks assign'd;
    All proud to serve their sov'reign's will.

5 Earth on her centre fix'd he set,
    Her face with water overspread;
Nor proudest mountains dar'd, as yet,
    To lift above the waves their head.

6 But when thy awful face appear'd,
    Th' insulting waves dispers'd; they fled,
When once thy thunder's voice they heard,
    And by their haste confess'd their dread.

7 Thence up by secret tracks they creep,
    And, gushing from the mountains side,
Thro' vallies travel to the deep
    Appointed to receive their tide.

PSALM VIII.

8 There haft thou fix'd the ocean's bounds,
  The threat'ning furges to repel;
 That they no more o'erpafs their mounds,
  Nor to a fecond deluge fwell.

9 Yet thence in fmaller parties drawn,
  The fea recovers her loft hills;
 And ftarting fprings, from ev'ry lawn,
  Surprife the vales with plenteous rills.

10 The fields' tame beafts are thither led,
  Weary with labour, faint with drought;
 And affes, on wild mountains bred,
  Have fenfe to find thefe currents out.

11 There fhady trees from fcorching beams,
  Yield fhelter to the feather'd throng;
 They drink, and to the bounteous ftreams
  Return the tribute of their fong.

12 His rains from heav'n parch'd hills recruit,
  That foon tranfmit the liquid ftore;
 'Till earth is burden'd with her fruit,
  And nature's lap can hold no more.

13 Grafs, for our cattle to devour,
  He makes the growth of every field;
 Herbs, for man's ufe, of various pow'r,
  That either food or phyfick yield.

14 With clufter'd grapes he crowns the vine,
  To cheer man's heart, opprefs'd with cares;
 Gives oil, that makes his face to fhine;
  And corn, that wafted ftrength repairs.

15 The trees of God, without the care
  Or art of man, with fap are fed;
 The mountain cedar looks as fair,
  As thofe in royal gardens bred.

16 Safe in the lofty cedar's arms
    The wand'rers of the air may rest;
The hospitable pine from harms
    Protects the stork, her pious guest.

17 Wild goats the craggy rock ascend,
    Its tow'ring heights their fortress make,
Whose cells in labyrinths extend,
    Where feebler creatures refuge take.

18 The moon's inconstant aspect shows
    Th' appointed seasons of the year;
Th' instructed sun his duty knows,
    His hours to rise and disappear.

19 Darkness he makes the earth to shroud,
    When forest-beasts securely stray;
Young lions roar their wants aloud
    To Providence, that sends them prey.

20 They range all night, on slaughter bent,
    'Till, summon'd by the rising morn
To skulk in dens, with one consent,
    The conscious ravagers return.

21 Forth to the tillage of his soil
    The husbandman securely goes,
Commencing with the sun his toil,
    With him returns to his repose.

22 How various, Lord, thy works are found!
    For which thy wisdom we adore!
The earth is with thy treasure crown'd,
    Till nature's hand can grasp no more.

23 But still the vast unfathom'd main
    Of wonders a new scene supplies,
Whose depths inhabitants contain
    Of ev'ry form and ev'ry size.

24 Full

24 Full freighted ships, from ev'ry port,
    There cut their unmolested way;
Leviathan, whom there to sport
    Thou mad'st, has compass there to play.

25 These various troops of sea and land
    In sense of common want agree;
All wait on thy dispensing hand,
    And have their daily alms from thee.

26 They gather what thy stores disperse,
    Without their trouble to provide;
Thou op'st thy hand, the universe,
    The craving world, is all supply'd.

27 Thou for a moment hid'st thy face,
    The num'rous ranks of creatures mourn:
Thou tak'st their breath, all nature's race
    Forthwith to mother earth return.

28 Again thou send'st thy spirit forth,
    T' inspire the mass with vital seed;
Nature's restor'd, and parent earth
    Smiles on her new created breed.

29 Thus through successive ages stands,
    Firm fix'd, thy providential care;
Pleas'd with the work of thine own hands,
    Thou dost the wastes of time repair.

30 In praising God, while he prolongs
    My breath, I will that breath employ;
And join devotion to my songs,
    Sincere as is in him my joy.

PSALM IX.

From the 111th of David.

1 PRAISE ye the Lord, our God to praise
   My soul her utmost pow'rs shall raise;
   With private friends, and in the throng
   Of saints, his praise shall be my song.

2 His works, for greatness tho' renown'd,
   His wond'rous works, with ease are found
   By those who seek for them aright,
   And in the pious search delight.

3 His works are all of matchless fame,
   And universal glory claim;
   His truth, confirm'd thro' ages past,
   Shall to eternal ages last.

4 By precept he has us enjoin'd,
   To keep his wond'rous works in mind;
   And to posterity record,
   That good and gracious is our Lord.

5 Just are the dealings of his hands;
   Immutable are his commands;
   By truth and equity sustain'd,
   And for eternal rules ordain'd.

6 Who wisdom's sacred prize would win,
   Must with the fear of God begin.
   Immortal praise and heav'nly skill
   Have they who know and do his will.

PSALM X.

From the 139th of David.

1. THOU, Lord, by strictest search hast known
My rising up and lying down:
My secret thoughts are known to thee,
Known long before conceiv'd by me.

2 Thine eye my bed and path surveys,
My publick haunts and private ways:
Thou know'st what 'tis my lips would vent,
My yet unutter'd words' intent.

3 Surrounded by thy pow'r I stand;
On ev'ry side I find thy hand.
O skill, for human reach too high!
Too dazzling bright for mortal eye!

4 Let me acknowledge, too, O God,
That since this maze of life I trod,
Thy thoughts of love to me surmount
The pow'r of numbers to recount:

5 Far sooner could I reckon o'er
The sands upon the ocean's shore:
Each morn, revising what I've done,
I find th' account but new begun.

6 Search, try, O God, my thoughts and heart,
If mischief lurks in any part;
Correct me where I go astray,
And guide me in thy perfect way.

PSALM XI.
From the 91st of David.

1 HE that has God his guardian made,
 Shall, under the Almighty's shade,
  Secure and undisturb'd abide.
 Thus to my soul of him I'll say,
 He is my fortress and my stay,
  My God, in whom I will confide.

2 His tender love and watchful care
 Shall free thee from the fowler's snare,
  And from the noisome pestilence;
 He over thee his wings shall spread,
 And cover thy unguarded head;
  His truth shall be thy strong defence.

3 No terrors, that surprize by night,
 Shall thy undaunted courage fright,
  Nor deadly shafts that fly by day;
 Nor plague, of unknown rise, that kills
 In darkness, nor infectious ills,
  That in the hottest season slay.

PSALM XII.
From the 113th of David.

1 YE saints and servants of the Lord,
 The triumphs of his name record:
  His sacred name forever bless.
 Where-e'er the circling sun displays
 His rising beams, or setting rays,
  Due praise to his great name address.

2 God through the world extends his sway:
The regions of eternal day
   But shadows of his glory are.
To him, whose majesty excels,
Who made the heav'n wherein he dwells,
   Let no created power compare.

FOURTH METRE.

PSALM XIII.
From the 25th of David.

1 THY mercies and thy love,
      O Lord, recal to mind;
   And graciously continue still,
      As thou wert ever, kind.

2 To me thy truth impart,
      And lead me in thy way:
   For thou art He that brings me help;
      On thee I wait all day.

3 Let all my youthful crimes
      Be blotted out by thee;
   And for thy wond'rous goodness sake,
      In mercy think on me.

4 His mercy and his truth,
      The righteous Lord displays,
   In bringing wand'ring sinners home,
      And teaching them his ways.

5 He those in justice guides,
      Who his direction seek;
   And in his sacred paths shall lead
      The humble and the meek.

6 Through

6 Through all the ways of God
    Both truth and mercy shine,
 To such as, with religious hearts,
    To his blest will incline.

FIFTH METRE.

PSALM XIV.

From the 149th of David:

1 O PRAISE ye the Lord, prepare a new song,
    And let all his saints in full chorus join;
 With voices united the anthem prolong,
 And shew forth his praises with musick divine.

2 Let praise to the Lord, who made us, ascend;
 Let each grateful heart be glad in its King;
 For God, whom we worship, our songs will attend,
 And view with complacence the offering we bring.

3 Be joyful, ye saints, sustain'd by his might,
 And let your glad songs awake with each morn;
 For those who obey him are still his delight;
 His hand with salvation the meek will adorn.

4 Then praise ye the Lord, prepare a glad song,
 And let all his saints in full chorus join;
 With voices united the anthem prolong,
 And shew forth his praises with musick divine.

PSALM XV.

SIXTH METRE.

PSALM XV.
From the 148th of David.

1 YE boundless realms of joy,
    Exalt your Maker's fame;
His praise your songs employ
    Above the starry frame;
      Your voices raise,
      Ye Cherubim
      And Seraphim,
      To sing his praise.

2 Thou moon that rul'st the night,
    And sun that guid'st the day;
Ye glitt'ring stars of light,
    To him your homage pay;
      His praise declare,
      Ye heav'ns above,
      And clouds that move
      In liquid air.

3 Let them adore the Lord,
    And praise his holy name,
By whose almighty word
    They all from nothing came:
      And all shall last,
      From changes free;
      His firm decree
      Stands ever fast.

4 United zeal be shown,
    His wond'rous fame to raise,
Whose glorious name alone
Deserves our endless praise.
      Earth's utmost ends
      His pow'r obey:
      His glorious sway
      The sky transcends.

SEVENTH METRE.

PSALM XVI.

From the 96th of David.

1 SING to the Lord a new made song:
    Let earth, in one assembled throng,
     Her common patron's praise resound;
  Sing to the Lord and bless his name,
  From day to day his praise proclaim,
     Who us has with salvation crown'd.
  To heathen lands his fame rehearse,
  His wonders to the universe.

2 He's great, and greatly to be prais'd;
  In majesty and glory rais'd
     Above all other deities;
  For pageantry and idols all
  Are they whom Gods the heathen call;
     He only rules who made the skies:
  With majesty and honour crown'd,
  Beauty and strength his throne surround.

3 Proclaim aloud, Jehovah reigns,
  Whose pow'r the universe sustains,
     And banish'd justice will restore:
  Let therefore heav'n new joys confess,
  And heav'nly mirth let earth express,
     Its loud applause the ocean roar;
  Its mute inhabitants rejoice,
  And for his triumph find a voice,

PSALMS *of* PRAYER, *suited to various Circumstances of Life.*

PSALM XVII.

From the 43d of David.

1 AS pants the hart for cooling streams,
   When heated in the chace,
So longs my soul, O God, for thee,
   And thy refreshing grace.

2 For thee, my God, the living God,
   My thirsty soul doth pine!
O when shall I behold thy face?
   Thou majesty divine!

3 I sigh whene'er my musing thoughts
   Those happy days present,
When I with troops of pious friends
   Thy temple did frequent;

4 When I advanc'd with songs of praise,
   My solemn vows to pay,
And led the joyful sacred throng
   That kept the festal day.

5 Why restless, why cast down, my soul?
   Trust God, and he'll employ
His aid for thee; and change these sighs
   To thankful hymns of joy.

6 Why restless, why cast down, my soul?
   Hope still, and thou shalt sing
The praise of him who is thy God,
   Thy health's eternal spring.

PSALM XVIII.

From the 84th of David.

1 O LORD of hosts, my King and God,
    How highly bleſt are they,
Who in thy temple always dwell,
    And there thy praiſe diſplay!

2 Thrice happy they, whoſe choice has thee
    Their ſure protection made;
Who long to tread the ſacred ways
    That to thy dwelling lead!

3 For in thy courts one ſingle day
    'Tis better to attend,
Than, Lord, in any place beſides
    A thouſand days to ſpend.

4 Much rather in God's houſe will I
    The meaneſt office take,
Than in the wealthy tents of ſin
    My pompous dwelling make.

5 For God, who is our ſun and ſhield,
    Will grace and glory give;
And no good thing will he withhold
    From them that juſtly live.

6 Thou, God, whom heav'nly hoſts obey,
    How highly bleſt is he,
Whoſe hope and truſt, ſecurely plac'd,
    Is ſtill repos'd on thee!

PSALM XIX.

From the 86th of David.

1 THOU Lord art good, not only good,
    But prompt to pardon too;
Of plenteous mercy to all those,
    Who for thy mercy sue.

2 To my repeated humble pray'r,
    O Lord, attentive be!
When troubled, I on thee will call,
    For thou wilt answer me.

3 Among the Gods there's none like thee,
    O Lord, alone divine!
To thee as much inferiour they,
    As are their works to thine.

4 Therefore their great Creator, thee,
    The nations shall adore;
Their long misguided pray'rs and praise
    To thy blest name restore.

5 All shall confess thee great, and great
    The wonders thou hast done;
Confess thee God, the God supreme,
    Confess thee God alone.

PSALM XX.

From the 90th of David.

1 O TO thy servants, Lord, return,
    And speedily relent!
As we of our misdeeds, do thou
    Of our just doom, repent.

2 To satisfy and cheer our souls,
    Thy early mercy send;
  That we may all our days to come
    In joy and comfort spend.

3 Let happy times, with large amends,
    Dry up our former tears;
  Or equal at the least the term
    Of our afflicted years.

4 To all thy servants, Lord, let this
    Thy wond'rous work be known,
  And to our offspring yet unborn,
    Thy glorious pow'r be shown.

5 Let thy bright rays upon us shine,
    Give thou our work success;
  The glorious work we have in hand
    Do thou vouchsafe to bless.

PSALM XXI.
From the 141st of David.

1 TO thee, O Lord, my cries ascend,
    O haste to my relief;
  And with accustom'd pity hear
    The accents of my grief.

2 Instead of off'rings, let my pray'r
    Like morning incense rise;
  My lifted hands supply the place
    Of ev'ning sacrifice.

3 From hasty language curb my tongue,
    And let a constant guard
  Still keep the portal of my lips
    With wary silence barr'd.

From wicked men's designs and deeds
  My heart and hands restrain:
Nor let me in the booty share
  Of their unrighteous gain.

Let upright men reprove my faults,
  And I shall think them kind;
Like balm that heals a wounded head,
  I their reproof shall find.

And in return, my fervent pray'r
  I shall for them address,
When they are tempted and reduc'd,
  Like me, to sore distress.

PSALM XXII.
From the 63d of David.

O GOD, my gracious God, to thee
  My morning pray'rs shall offer'd be;
For thee my thirsty soul does pant;
My fainting flesh implores thy grace,
Within this dry and barren place,
  Where I refreshing waters want.

My life, while I that life enjoy,
In blessing God I will employ,
  With lifted hands adore his name:
My soul's content shall be as great,
As theirs who choicest dainties eat,
  While I with joy his praise proclaim.

When I lie down, sweet sleep to find,
Thou, Lord, art present to my mind,
  And when I wake in dead of night:
Because thou still dost succour bring,
Beneath the shadow of thy wing,
  I rest with safety and delight.

PSALM XXIII.

From the 67th of David.

1 TO bless thy chosen race,
   In mercy, Lord, incline ;
And cause the brightness of thy face
   On all thy saints to shine :

2 That so thy wond'rous way
   May through the world be known ;
Whilst distant lands their tribute pay,
   And thy salvation own.

3 Let diff'ring nations join
   To celebrate thy fame ;
Let all the world, O Lord, combine
   To praise thy glorious name.

4 O let them shout and sing,
   Dissolv'd in pious mirth ;
For thou, the righteous Judge and King,
   Shalt govern all the earth.

5 Let diff'ring nations join,
   To celebrate thy fame ;
Let all the world, O Lord, combine
   To praise thy glorious name.

PSALMS of THANKSGIVING.

PSALM XXIV.

From the 22d of David.

1 TO all my brethren I'll declare
    The triumphs of God's name;
In presence of assembled saints,
    His glory I'll proclaim.

2 'Tis his supreme prerogative
    O'er subject kings to reign;
'Tis just that he should rule the world,
    Who does the world sustain.

3 The rich, who are with plenty fed,
    His bounty must confess;
The sons of want, by him reliev'd,
    Their gen'rous patron bless.

4 With humble worship, to his throne
    They all for aid resort:
That pow'r, which first their beings gave,
    Can only them support.

PSALM XXV.

From the 23d of David.

1 THE Lord himself, the mighty Lord,
    Vouchsafes to be my guide;
The shepherd by whose constant care
    My wants are all supply'd.

2 In tender grass he makes me feed,
    And gently there repose;
Then leads me to cool shades, and where
    Refreshing water flows.

3 He does my wand'ring foul reclaim;
    And, to his endlefs praife,
Inftructs with humble zeal to walk
    In his moft righteous ways.

4 I pafs the gloomy vale of death
    From fear and danger free;
For there his aiding rod and ftaff
    Defend and comfort me.

PSALM XXVI.

From the 108th of David.

1 O GOD, my heart is fully bent,
    To magnify thy name;
My tongue, with cheerful fongs of praife,
    Shall celebrate thy fame.

2 To all the lift'ning tribes, O Lord,
    Thy wond'rous works I'll tell;
And to thofe nations fing thy praife,
    That round about us dwell:

3 Becaufe thy mercy's boundlefs height
    The higheft heav'n tranfcends;
And far beyond th' afpiring clouds
    Thy faithful truth extends.

4 Be thou, O God, exalted high
    Above the ftarry frame;
And let the world, with one confent,
    Confefs thy glorious name.

PSALM XXVII.

From the 18th of David.

1 THOU suit'st, O Lord, thy righteous ways
 To various paths of human kind;
They who for mercy merit praise,
 With thee shall wond'rous mercy find.

2 Thou to the just shall justice show,
 The pure thy purity shall see;
Such as perversely choose to go,
 Shall meet with due returns from thee.

3 For God's designs shall still succeed;
 His word will bear the utmost test:
He's a strong shield to all that need,
 And on his sure protection rest.

4 Who then deserves to be ador'd,
 But God, on whom my hopes depend?
Or who, except the mighty Lord,
 Can with resistless pow'r defend?

5 Therefore, to celebrate his fame,
 My grateful voice to heav'n I'll raise;
And nations, strangers to his name,
 Shall thus be taught to sing his praise.

PSALM XXVIII.

From the 103d of David.

1 THE Lord abounds with tender love,
 And unexampled acts of grace;
His waken'd wrath does slowly move,
 His willing mercy flows apace.

2 God will not always harshly chide,
    But with his anger quickly part;
And loves his punishments to guide,
    More by his love than our desert.

3 As high as heav'n its arch extends
    Above this little spot of clay,
So much his boundless love transcends
    The small respects that we can pay.

4 As far as 'tis from east to west,
    So far has he our sins remov'd;
Who, with a father's tender breast,
    Has such as fear him always lov'd.

PSALM XXIX.

From the 106th of David.

1 O RENDER thanks to God above,
    The fountain of eternal love;
Whose mercy firm through ages past
Has stood, and shall forever last.

2 Who can his mighty deeds express,
Not only vast but numberless?
What mortal eloquence can raise
His tribute of immortal praise?

3 Happy are they, and only they,
Who from thy judgments never stray:
Who know what's right, not only so,
But always practise what they know.

4 O may I worthy prove to see
Thy saints in full prosperity!
That I the joyful choir may join,
And count thy people's triumph mine.

PSALM

PSALM XXX.

From the 107th of David.

1. THEY that in ships, with courage bold,
    O'er swelling waves their trade pursue,
Do God's amazing works behold,
    And in the deep his wonders view!

2 No sooner his command is past,
    But forth a dreadful tempest flies,
Which sweeps the sea with rapid b'ast,
    And makes the stormy billows rise.

3 Sometimes the ships, toss'd up to heav'n,
    On tops of mountain waves appear;
Then down the steep abyss are driv'n,
    Whilst ev'ry soul dissolves with fear.

4 They reel and stagger to and fro,
    Like men with fumes of wine oppress'd;
Nor do the skilful seamen know
    Which way to steer, what course is best.

5 Then strait to God's indulgent ear
    They do their mournful cry address,
Who graciously vouchsafes to hear,
    And frees them from their deep distress.

6 He does the raging storm appease,
    And makes the billows calm and still;
With joy they see their fury cease,
    And their intended course fulfil.

7 O then that all the earth, with me,
    Would God for this his goodness praise!
And for the mighty works which he
    Thro' all the wond'ring world displays!

PSALM

PSALM XXXI.

From the 150th of David.

1 O PRAISE the Lord in that bleſt place,
    From whence his goodneſs largely flows;
Praiſe him in heav'n, where he his face
    Unveil'd in perfect glory ſhows.

2 Praiſe him for all the mighty acts
    Which he in our behalf has done;
His kindneſs this return exacts,
    With which our praiſe ſhould equal run.

3 Let the ſhrill trumpet's warlike voice
    Make rocks and hills his praiſe rebound;
Praiſe him with harp's melodious noiſe,
    And gentle pſaltry's ſilver ſound.

4 Let virgin troops ſoft timbrels bring,
    And ſome with graceful motion dance;
Let inſtruments of various ſtrings,
    With organs join'd, his praiſe advance.

5 Let them who joyful hymns compoſe,
    To cymbals ſet their ſongs of praiſe;
Cymbals of common uſe, and thoſe
    That loudly ſound on ſolemn days.

6 Let all that vital breath enjoy,
    The breath he does to them afford,
In juſt returns of praiſe employ;
    Let every creature praiſe the Lord.

PSALM XXXII.

From the 136th of David.

1 TO God, the mighty Lord,
 Your joyful thanks repeat:
To him due praise afford,
As good as he is great.
  For God does prove
  Our constant friend,
  His boundless love
  Shall never end.

2 To him whose wond'rous pow'r
All other gods obey,
Whom earthly kings adore,
This grateful homage pay.
  For God, &c.

3 By his Almighty hand
Amazing works are wrought;
The heav'ns by his command
Were to perfection brought.
  For God, &c.

4 He does the food supply,
On which all creatures live:
To God who reigns on high
Eternal praises give.
  For God will prove
  Our constant friend,
  His boundless love
  Shall never end.

INSTRUCTIVE PSALMS.

PSALM XXXIII.

From the 1st of David.

1 HOW bleſt is he, who ne'er conſents
    By ill advice to walk;
  Nor ſtands in ſinners' ways, nor ſits
    Where men profanely talk:

2 But makes the perfect law of God
    His buſ'neſs and delight;
  Devoutly reads therein by day,
    And meditates by night.

3 Like ſome fair tree, which, fed by ſtreams,
    With timely fruit does bend,
  He ſtill ſhall flouriſh, and ſucceſs
    All his deſigns attend.

4 Ungodly men, and their attempts,
    No laſting root ſhall find;
  Untimely blaſted, and diſpers'd
    Like chaff before the wind.

5 For God approves the juſt man's ways;
    To happineſs they tend:
  But ſinners, and the paths they tread,
    Shall both in ruin end.

PSALM XXXIV.

From the 4th of David.

1 CONSIDER that the righteous man
    Is God's peculiar choice:
  And when to him I make my pray'r,
    He always hears my voice.

2 Then stand in awe of his commands;
   Flee ev'ry thing that's ill;
Commune in private with your hearts,
   And bend them to his will.

3 The place of other sacrifice
   Let righteousness supply:
And let your hope, securely fix'd,
   On God alone rely.

4 While worldly minds impatient grow,
   More prosp'rous times to see;
Still let the glories of thy face
   Shine brightly, Lord, on me.

5 So shall my heart o'erflow with joy
   More lasting and more true,
Than theirs, who stores of corn and wine
   Successively renew.

6 Then down in peace I'll lay my head,
   And take my needful rest;
No other guard, O Lord, I crave,
   Of thy defence possess'd.

PSALM XXXV.
From the 15th of David.

1 LORD, who's the happy man, that may
     To thy blest courts repair;
And, while he bows before thy throne,
   Shall find acceptance there?

2 'Tis he, whose ev'ry thought and deed
   By rules of virtue moves;
Whose gen'rous tongue disdains to speak
   The thing his heart disproves:

3 Who

3 Who never did a slander forge,
  His neighbour's fame to wound;
Nor hearken to a false report,
  By malice whisper'd round:

4 Who vice, in all its pomp and pow'r,
  Can treat with just neglect;
And piety, though cloth'd in rags,
  Religiously respect:

5 Who to his plighted vows and trust
  Has ever firmly stood;
And, though he promise to his loss,
  He makes his promise good:

6 Who seeks not by oppressive ways
  His treasure to employ;
Whom no rewards can ever bribe,
  The guiltless to destroy.

7 The man, who, by this steady course,
  Has happiness ensur'd,
When earth's foundation shakes, shall stand,
  By Providence secur'd.

PSALM XXXVI.
From the 19th of David.

1 GOD's perfect law converts the soul,
   Reclaims from false desires;
With sacred wisdom his sure word
  The ignorant inspires.

2 The statutes of the Lord are just,
  And bring sincere delight:
His pure commands, in search of truth,
  Assist the feeblest sight.

3 His perfect worship here is fix'd,
    On sure foundations laid:
His equal laws are in the scales
    Of truth and justice weigh'd.

4 Of more esteem than golden mines,
    Or gold refin'd with skill;
More sweet than honey, or the drops
    That from the comb distil.

5 But what frail man observes how oft
    He does from virtue fall?
O! cleanse me from my secret faults,
    Thou, God, that know'st them all.

PSALM XXXVII.
From the 34th of David.

1 APPROACH, ye piously dispos'd,
    And my instruction hear;
I'll teach you the true discipline
    Of a religious fear.

2 Let him, who length of life desires,
    And prosp'rous ways would see,
From sland'ring language keep his tongue,
    His lips from falshood free:

3 The crooked paths of vice decline,
    And virtue's ways pursue;
Establish peace, where 'tis begun,
    And, where 'tis lost, renew.

4 The Lord, from heav'n, beholds the just
    With favourable eyes;
And, when distress'd, his gracious ear
    Is open to their cries:

5 But turns his wrathful look on those
    Whom mercy can't reclaim,
To cut them off, and from the earth
    Blot out their hated name.

PSALM XXXVIII.
From the 119th of David.

1 HOW bless'd are they who always keep
    The pure and perfect way!
Who never from the sacred paths
    Of God's commandment's stray!

2 Thrice bless'd! who to his righteous laws
    Have still obedient been!
And have, with fervent, humble zeal,
    His favour sought to win!

3 Such men their utmost caution use,
    To shun each wicked deed;
But in the path which he directs
    With constant care proceed.

4 Thou strictly hast enjoin'd us, Lord,
    To learn thy sacred will;
And all our diligence employ
    Thy statutes to fulfil.

5 O then that thy most holy will
    Might o'er my ways preside!
And I the course of all my life
    By thy direction guide!

6 Then with assurance would I walk,
    From all confusion free;
Convinc'd, with joy, that all my ways
    With thy commands agree.

7 The wonders, which thy law contains,
    No words can represent :
Therefore, to learn and practise them
    My zealous heart is bent.

8 The very entrance to thy word
    Celestial light displays,
And knowledge of true happiness
    To simplest minds conveys.

9 With eager hopes, I waiting stood,
    And fainted with desire,
That of thy wise commands I might
    The sacred skill acquire.

10 With favour, Lord, look down on me,
    Who thy relief implore ;
As thou art wont to visit those
    That thy blest name adore.

11 Directed by thy heav'nly word
    Let all my footsteps be ;
Nor wickedness, of any kind,
    Dominion have o'er me.

12 Forever and forever, Lord,
    Unchang'd thou dost remain ;
Thy word, establish'd in the heav'ns,
    Does all their orbs sustain.

13 Thro' circling ages, Lord, thy truth
    Immoveable shall stand ;
As doth the earth, which thou uphold'st
    By thy almighty hand.

14. All things the course by thee ordain'd,
    E'en to this day, fulfil ;
They are thy faithful subjects all,
    And servants of thy will.

15 Unless thy sacred law had been
    My comfort and delight,
  I must have fainted and expir'd
    In dark affliction's night.

16 Thy precepts, therefore, from my thoughts
    Shall never, Lord, depart;
  For thou by them hast to new life
    Restor'd my dying heart.

17 I've seen an end of what we call
    Perfection here below;
  But thy commandments, like thyself,
    No change or period know.

PSALM XXXIX.
From the 36th of David.

1 O LORD, thy mercy, my sure hope,
    The highest orb of heav'n transcends,
  Thy sacred truth's unmeasur'd scope
    Beyond the spreading sky extends.

2 Thy justice like the hills remains;
    Unfathom'd depths thy judgments are;
  Thy providence the world sustains,
    The whole creation is thy care.

3 Since of thy goodness all partake,
    With what assurance shall the just
  Thy shelt'ring wings their refuge make,
    And saints to thy protection trust!

4 Such guests shall to thy courts be led,
    To banquet on thy love's repast,
  And drink, as from a fountain's head,
    Of joys that shall forever last.

5 With thee the springs of life remain,
   Thy presence is eternal day:
O let thy saints thy favour gain:
   To upright hearts thy truth display.

PSALM XL.
From the 62d of David.

1 GOD does his saving health dispense,
     And flowing blessings daily send.
  He is my fortress and defence;
     On him my soul shall still depend.

2 In him, ye people, always trust;
     Before his throne pour out your hearts:
  For God, the merciful and just,
     His timely aid to us imparts.

3 The vulgar fickle are, and frail;
     The great dissemble and betray;
  And, laid in truth's impartial scale,
     The lightest things will both outweigh.

4 Then trust not in oppressive ways;
     By spoil and rapine grow not vain;
  Nor let your hearts, if wealth increase,
     Be set too much upon your gain.

5 For God has oft his will express'd,
     And I this truth have fully known;
  To be of boundless pow'r possess'd,
     Belongs, of right, to God alone.

6 Tho' mercy is his darling grace,
     In which he chiefly takes delight;
  Yet will he all the human race
     According to their works requite.

HYMNS.

HYMN I.

Religious Inquiry.

1 ALL knowing God, 'tis thine to know
 The springs whence wrong opinions flow;
 To judge, from principles within,
 When frailty errs, and when we sin.

2 Who, among men, high Lord of all,
 Thy servants to his bar may call?
 Decide of heresy, and shake
 A brother o'er the flaming lake?

3 Who with another's eye can read?
 Or worship by another's creed?
 Revering thy command alone,
 We humbly seek and use our own.

4 If wrong, forgive; accept, if right;
 While faithful we obey our light;
 And, cens'ring none, are zealous still,
 To follow as to learn thy will.

5 When shall our happy eyes behold
 Thy people fashion'd in thy mould?
 And charity our lineage prove
 Deriv'd from thee, O God of love?

HYMN II.

The Heavens declare the Glory of God.

1 THE spacious firmament on high,
   With all the blue ethereal sky,
   And spangled heav'ns (a shining frame!)
   Their Great Original proclaim.

2 Th' unwearied sun, from day to day,
   Does his Creator's pow'r display,
   And publishes, to ev'ry land,
   The work of an Almighty Hand.

3 Soon as the ev'ning shades prevail,
   The moon takes up the wond'rous tale,
   And nightly to the list'ning earth
   Repeats the story of her birth:

4 Whilst all the stars that round her burn,
   And all the planets in their turn,
   Confirm the tidings as they roll,
   And spread the truth from pole to pole.

5 What though, in solemn silence, all
   Move round the dark terrestrial ball?
   What though nor real voice nor sound
   Amid their radiant orbs be found?

6 In Reason's ear they all rejoice,
   And utter forth a glorious voice;
   Forever singing, as they shine,
   "The Hand that made us is divine."

HYMN III.
To the one only true God.

1. ETERNAL God, Almighty Cause
    Of earth, and seas, and worlds unknown!
  All things are subject to thy laws,
    All things depend on thee alone.

2. Thy glorious being firmly stands,
    Of all within itself possest;
  Controul'd by none are thy commands,
    Thou from thyself alone art blest.

3. To thee alone ourselves we owe,
    To thee alone our homage pay;
  All other Gods we disavow,
    Deny their claims, renounce their sway.

4. Spread thy great name thro' every land,
    Each idol deity dethrone,
  Let earth with all her tongues confess
    That thou the Lord art God alone.

HYMN IV.
Devotion.

1. BEFORE Jehovah's awful throne,
    Ye nations, bow, with sacred joy:
  Know that the Lord is God alone;
    He can create, and he destroy.

2. His sov'reign pow'r, without our aid,
    Made us of clay, and form'd us men;
  And when like wand'ring sheep we stray'd,
    He brought us to his fold again.

3 Wide as the world is thy command,
    Vast as eternity thy love!
Firm as a rock thy truth shall stand,
    When rolling years shall cease to move.

4 We'll crowd thy gates with thankful songs,
    High as the heav'ns our voices raise;
And earth, with her ten thousand tongues,
    Shall fill thy courts with sounding praise.

HYMN V.
The Wisdom of God.

1 IN all our Maker's vast designs
    Lo! his eternal wisdom shines;
Through all creation spread abroad,
Loud it proclaims the Maker, God.

2 With rev'rence our admiring eyes
    Survey thy wonders in the skies;
Thy wisdom round the world we see,
The spacious earth is full of thee.

3 Above the earth, beyond the sky,
    Stands thy high throne of majesty;
Nor time nor place thy power restrain,
Nor bound thy universal reign.

4 Amazing knowledge, vast and great!
    What large extent, what lofty height!
Our souls, with all the powers they boast,
Are in the boundless prospect lost.

5 Lord, who can speak thy wond'rous deeds?
    Thy wisdom all our thoughts exceeds;
Vast and unsearchable thy ways,
Vast and immortal be thy praise.

HYMN VI.
The Justice of God.

1 GREAT God, to thee, the mighty King,
    Whose sovereign rule the world obeys,
With reverent hearts thy people bring
    The tribute of their humble praise.

2 The earth's great sceptre fills thy hand;
    And, high enthron'd in majesty,
Thou givest thence to every land
    The laws of truth and equity.

2 Unerring justice, Lord, is thine;
    And every nation shall confess,
That thy decrees are all divine,
    And all thy ways are righteousness.

4 In judgment wise, thou wilt bestow
    To every soul its due reward;
Unceasing joy the good shall know,
    And live forever with their Lord.

5 But they who tread the sinner's path,
    And dare thy righteous laws disown,
Shall meet with due returns from thee,
    And reap the fruit which they have sown.

HYMN VII.
The Mercy of God.

1 O THOU, the wretched's sure retreat,
    Who dost their cares controul,
And with the cheerful smile of peace
    Revive the fainting soul!

2 Did ever thy relenting ear
   The humble plea difdain?
Or when did plaintive mifery figh,
   Or fupplicate, in vain?

3 Whoe'er to thee for pardon fue
   In penitential tears,
Thy goodnefs calms their reftlefs doubts,
   And diffipates their fears.

4 New life from thy refrefhing grace,
   Their finking hearts receive;
Thy gentleft, beft-lov'd attribute,
   To pity and forgive.

5 From that bleft fource propitious hope
   Appears ferenely bright,
And fheds her foft diffufive beam
   O'er forrow's difmal night.

6 Our griefs confefs her vital power,
   And blefs the friendly ray,
Which ufhers in the fmiling morn
   Of everlafting day.

HYMN VIII.

The Greatnefs and Majefty of God.

1 THE Lord of glory reigns; he reigns on high;
      His robes of ftate are ftrength and majefty;
   This wide creation rofe at his command;
   Built by his word, and 'ftablifh'd by his hand:
Long ftood his throne, 'ere he began creation,
And his own Godhead is the firm foundation.

2 God is th' eternal King : Thy foes in vain
  Raise their rebellion to confound thy reign :
  In vain the storms, in vain the floods arise,
  And roar, and toss their waves against the skies ;
Foaming at heav'n, they rage with wild commotion,
But heav'n's high arches scorn the swelling ocean.

3 Ye tempests, rage no more ! ye floods, be still !
  And the mad world submissive to his will !
  Built on his truth, his church must ever stand :
  Firm are his promises, and strong his hand :
See his own sons, when they appear before him,
Bow at his footstool, and with fear adore him !

HYMN IX.
To God the Creator.

1 ALMIGHTY Maker, God !
    How wond'rous is thy name !
  Thy glories how diffus'd abroad
    Through all creation's frame !

2 Nature, in ev'ry dress,
    Her humble homage pays ;
  And does a thousand ways express
    Her undissembled praise.

3 Our souls would rise and sing
    Our Great Creator, too ;
  Fain would our tongues adore our King,
    And pay the homage due.

4 Let joy and worship spend
    The remnant of our days,
  And oft to God our souls ascend
    In grateful songs of praise.

HYMN

HYMN X.
God known by his Works.

1 GREAT God! the heav'ns well-order'd frame
  Declares the glories of thy name;
    There thy rich works of wonder shine;
  A thousand starry beauties there,
  A thousand radiant marks appear,
    Of boundless pow'r, and skill divine.

2 From night to day, from day to night,
  The dawning and the dying light,
    Lectures of heav'nly wisdom read;
  With silent eloquence they raise
  Our thoughts to the Creator's praise,
    And neither sound nor language need.

3 Yet their divine instructions run
  Far as the journeys of the sun;
    All nature joins to shew thy praise:
  Thus God in every creature shines;
  Fair is the book of nature's lines,
    Which shews thy wisdom and thy grace.

HYMN XI.
The Voice of Nature.

1 THERE is a God, all nature speaks,
    Thro' earth, and air, and seas, and skies;
  See, from the clouds his glory breaks,
    When the first beams of morning rise.

2 The rising sun, serenely bright,
    O'er the wide world's extended frame,
  Inscribes, in characters of light,
    His mighty Maker's glorious name.

3 Diffusing

3 Diffusing life, his influence spreads;
  And health and plenty smile around;
And fruitful fields, and verdant meads,
  Are with a thousand blessings crown'd.

4 The flow'ry tribes, all blooming, rise
  Above the weak attempts of art;
Their bright, inimitable dyes
  Speak sweet conviction to the heart.

5 Ye curious minds, who roam abroad,
  And trace creation's wonders o'er;
Confess the footsteps of the God,
  And bow before him, and adore.

HYMN XII.
The God of Nature and Providence.

1 JOIN, every tongue, to praise the Lord:
  All nature rests upon his word:
His works proclaim his power divine;
O'er all the earth his glories shine.

2 Seasons and times obey his voice;
The ev'ning and the morn rejoice,
To see the earth made soft with show'rs,
Laden with fruit, and dress'd in flow'rs.

3 'Tis from his wat'ry stores on high,
He gives the thirsty ground supply;
He walks upon the clouds, and thence
Doth his enriching drops dispense.

4 The desert grows a fruitful field;
Abundant fruit the meadows yield;
The vallies shout with cheerful voice,
And neighb'ring hills repeat their joys.

5 Thy

5 Thy works pronounce thy pow'r divine;
In all the earth thy glories shine;
Through ev'ry month thy gifts appear;
Great God! thy goodness crowns the year.

HYMN XIII.

The Providence of God in the Seasons of the Year.

1 ETERNAL Source of ev'ry joy!
Well may thy praise our lips employ,
While in thy temple we appear
To hail thee Sovereign of the year.

2 Wide as the wheels of nature roll,
Thy hand supports and guides the whole;
The sun is taught by thee to rise,
And darkness, when to veil the skies.

3 The flow'ry spring, at thy command,
Perfumes the air, and paints the land;
The summer rays with vigour shine,
To raise the corn and cheer the vine.

4 Thy hand, in autumn, richly pours,
Through all our coasts, redundant stores;
And winters, soften'd by thy care,
No more the face of horror wear.

5 Seasons, and months, and weeks, and days,
Demand successive songs of praise:
And be the grateful homage paid,
With morning light and ev'ning shade.

HYMN XIV.

The Bounty of God in the Works of Creation.

1 WE bless the Lord, the great, the good,
   Who fills our hearts with joy and food;
 Who pours his blessings from the skies,
 And loads our days with rich supplies.

2 He sends the sun his circuit round,
   To cheer the fruits and warm the ground;
 In plenteous drops his genial rain
 Revives the grass and swells the grain.

3 His bounteous hand, Great Spring of Good,
 Provides the whole creation food;
 He ever gives, yet still has more;
 His gifts can ne'er decrease his store.

4 We bless the Lord who reigns above,
 Whose thoughts are kind, whose name is love;
 Whose bounty through creation flows,
 And life and bliss on all bestows.

5 O let our souls with joy record
 The pow'r and goodness of the Lord;
 How great his works, how kind his ways!
 Let ev'ry tongue pronounce his praise.

HYMN XV.

Thanks to God for his bounteous Provision.

1 PRAISE to God, immortal praise,
   For the love that crowns our days!
 Bounteous Source of ev'ry joy,
 Let thy praise our tongues employ;

For the blessings of the field;
  For the stores the gardens yield;
  For the vine's exalted juice;
  For the gen'rous olive's use;

3 Flocks, that whiten all the plain;
  Yellow sheaves of ripen'd grain;
  Clouds, that drop their fatt'ning dews;
  Suns, that temp'rate warmth diffuse;

4 All that spring, with bounteous hand,
  Scatters o'er the smiling land;
  All that lib'ral autumn pours
  From her rich, o'erflowing stores.

5 These to thee, great God, we owe;
  Source, whence all our blessings flow:
  And for these our souls shall raise
  Grateful vows and solemn praise.

HYMN XVI.

The Goodness of God to all his Creatures.

1 WE bless the God whose bounteous love
    Through all creation flows;
  Who pours his blessings from above,
    And life and bliss bestows.

2 God reigns on high, but not confines
    His goodness to the skies;
  Through the whole earth his bounty shines,
    And every want supplies.

3 With longing eyes his creatures wait
    On him for daily food;
  His lib'ral hand provides them meat,
    And fills their hearts with good.

4 Benign

4 Benign Creator! bounteous Lord!
  Where'er we turn our eyes,
Fruits of thy wisdom, pow'r, and love,
  In beauteous order rise.

5 Then let our cheerful hearts and tongues
  Proclaim the praise divine:
Thou, Lord, hast given the rich increase,
  And be the glory thine.

HYMN XVII.
The peculiar Goodness of God to Mankind.

1 O LORD, how glorious is thy name,
  Through the wide earth's extended frame!
Majestick glories form thy seat,
And heaven adores beneath thy feet.

2 When all thy shining works on high
We meditate with raptur'd eye;
The silver moon, the starry train,
Which gild the fair etherial plain:

3 Lord, what is man, that he should share
Thy notice, thy indulgent care?
That man, frail child of earth, should be
The favourite of the Deity?

4 His place, thy forming hand assign'd,
But just below th' angelick kind;
With noblest favours circled round,
And with distinguish'd honours crown'd,

5 Invested him with power and sway,
And bid the subject brutes obey;
Sovereign of all thy works below,
To him the meaner creatures bow;

6 The bleating flocks, the lowing herds,
   The gliding fish, the flying birds;
   All that the earth's wide circuit yields,
   Natives of air, or seas, or fields.

7 But still let man, adoring, own
   That Thou, O Lord, art King alone;
   And through the earth's extended frame
   Declare the glories of thy name.

HYMN XVIII.
Praise to God for his Wonderful Works.

1 YE sons of men, with joy record
   The various wonders of the Lord;
   And let his power and goodness sound
   Through all your tribes the earth around.

2 Let the high heavens your songs invite,
   Those spacious fields of brilliant light;
   Where sun, and moon, and planets roll,
   And stars, that glow from pole to pole.

3 Sing, earth, in verdant robes array'd,
   Its herbs and flowers, its fruit and shade;
   Peopled with life of various forms,
   Of fish, and fowl, and beasts, and worms.

4 View the broad sea's majestick plains,
   And think how wide its Maker reigns;
   That band remotest nations joins,
   And on each wave his goodness shines.

5 Ye sons of men, with joy record
   The various wonders of the Lord;
   And let his power and goodness found
   Through all your tribes the earth around.

6 Praise ye the Lord; our hearts shall join
   In work so pleasant, so divine;
   Our days of praise shall ne'er be past,
   While life, and thought, and being last.

HYMN XIX.
The Beauties of Nature.

1 HOW cheerful along the gay mead
      The daisies and cowslips appear;
   The flocks, as they carelesly feed,
      Rejoice in the spring of the year.

2 The foliage that shades the gay bowers,
      The herbage that springs from the clod,
   Trees, plants, cooling fruits, and fair flow'rs,
      All rise to the praise of our God.

3 Shall man, the great master of all,
      The only insensible prove?
   Forbid it fair gratitude's call,
      Forbid it devotion and love.

4 The God who such wonders can raise,
      Forever his name be ador'd;
   Our lips shall incessantly praise,
      Our heart shall rejoice in the Lord.

HYMN XX.
The Wisdom of God in his Works.

1 SONGS of immortal praise belong
      To thee, Almighty God;
   To thee are due our heart, our tongue,
      To spread thy name abroad.

2 How great the works thy hand has wrought!
　　How glorious in our sight!
　And men in ev'ry age have sought
　　Thy wonders with delight.

3 How most exact is nature's frame!
　　How wise th' Eternal Mind!
　Thy counsels never change the scheme
　　Which thy first thoughts design'd.

4 Nature, and time, and earth, and skies,
　　Thy heav'nly skill proclaim;
　What shall we do to make us wise,
　　But learn to read thy name?

5 To fear thy pow'r, to trust thy grace,
　　Is our divinest skill;
　And he's the wisest of our race,
　　Who best obeys thy will.

HYMN XXI.

All Nations invoked to praise the Creator.

1 YE nations round the earth, rejoice
　　Before the Lord, your sov'reign King;
　Serve him with cheerful heart and voice;
　　With all your tongues his glory sing.

2 The Lord is God; 'tis he alone
　　Doth life, and breath, and being, give;
　We are his work, and not our own;
　　The sheep that on his pastures live.

3 Enter his gates with songs of joy,
　　With praises to his courts repair;
　And make it your divine employ
　　To pay your thanks and honours there.

4 The Lord is good, the Lord is kind;
  Great is his grace, his mercy sure;
  And the whole race of man shall find
  His truth from age to age endure.

HYMN XXII.

An Invocation to praise God our Creator.

1 LIFT your voice, and thankful sing
    Praises to our Heavenly King.
  Be the Lord your only theme,
  Who of Gods is God supreme;
  For his blessings far extend,
  And his mercy knows no end.

2 He asserts his just command,
  By the wonders of his hand,
  He whose wisdom thron'd on high,
  Built the mansions of the sky;
  For his blessings far extend,
  And his mercy knows no end.

3 He who bade the watery deep,
  Under earth's foundation sleep;
  And the orbs that gild the pole,
  Through the boundless ether roll;
  For his blessings far extend,
  And his mercy knows no end.

4 Thou, O sun, whose powerful ray
  Rules the empire of the day;
  You, O moon and stars, whose light
  Gilds the darkness of the night:
  For his blessings far extend,
  And his mercy knows no end.

5 He with food sustains, O earth,
All who claim from thee their birth;
Yield the homage that his name
From a creature's lips may claim:
For his blessings far extend,
And his mercy knows no end.

HYMN XXIII.

Praise to God, our Creator and Preserver.

1 GIVE to our God immortal praise!
Mercy and truth are all his ways:
Wonders of grace to God belong;
Repeat his mercies in your song.

2 Give to the Lord of Lords renown;
The King of Kings with glory crown:
His mercies ever shall endure,
When Lords and Kings are known no more.

3 He built the earth; he spread the sky,
And fix'd the starry lights on high:
Wonders of grace to God belong,
Repeat his mercies in your song.

4 He fills the sun with morning light;
And bids the moon direct the night:
His mercies ever shall endure,
When suns and moons shall be no more.

5 Give to our God immortal praise,
Mercy and truth are all his ways:
Wonders of grace to God belong,
Repeat his mercies in your song.

6 Through this vain world he guides our feet,
And leads us to his heav'nly seat:
His mercies ever shall endure,
When this vain world shall be no more.

HYMN XXIV.
All Nature invoked to praise the Creator.

1 YE bless'd inhabitants of heaven,
   To God be all your praises given;
O praise him in the realms that lie
Above the reach of mortal eye.

2 Praise him, thou sun, that round the pole
With restless course art seen to roll;
Ye moon and stars, his praise repeat;
Praise him, ye heav'ns, his awful seat.

3 Nor let the heav'ns his praise confine:
O, all of earth, the chorus join;
Ye beasts, that range th' uncultur'd soil,
Or patient lend to man your toil.

4 Praise him, each bird that wings the air,
Each reptile, nurtur'd by his care;
And every wind, and every storm,
That duteous his commands perform.

5 Ye youthful bands, and virgin choir,
Each lisping babe, and hoary sire,
Wake to his name your grateful songs;
To him alone all praise belongs.

6 His glory earth's wide bounds o'erflows,
Nor highest heav'n its limit knows:
O come, your thankful voices raise,
And consecrate to him your praise.

HYMN

HYMN XXV.

All Nature invoked to praise the Creator.

1 LET ev'ry creature join
    To praise th' eternal God:
Ye heav'nly hosts, the song begin,
    And sound his name abroad.

2   Thou sun with golden beams,
    And moon with paler rays,
Ye starry lights, ye heav'nly flames,
    Shine to your Maker's praise.

3   Ye vapours, when ye rise,
    Or fall in show'rs or snow;
Ye thunders, murm'ring round the skies,
    His pow'r and glory show.

4   Wind, hail, and flashing fire,
    Agree to praise the Lord,
When ye in dreadful storms conspire
    To execute his word.

5   Let earth and ocean know,
    They owe their Maker praise:
Praise him, ye wat'ry worlds below,
    Ye natives of the seas.

6   Monarchs of wide command,
    Praise ye th' eternal King;
Judges, adore that sov'reign hand,
    Whence all your honours spring.

7   United zeal be shown,
    His wond'rous fame to raise;
God is the Lord; his name alone
    Deserves our endless praise.

HYMN XXVI.

All Nature invoked to praise the Creator.

1 O For an hymn of universal praise!
   Its Maker's fame let ev'ry creature raise;
   Ye glorious angels tune the raptur'd lay
   Thro' the fair mansions of eternal day;
   His praise let all your shining ranks proclaim,
   And teach the distant worlds your Maker's name.

2 His glorious power, O radiant sun, display
   Far as thy cheering beams diffuse the day;
   Ye moon and stars, array'd in softer light,
   Recount his wonders to the list'ning night;
   His power, ye fair expanded skies, proclaim,
   Whose word produc'd the vast stupendous frame.

3 Let earth adore the universal Lord;
   Through ev'ry land be his great name ador'd;
   While loud his praises foaming billows roar,
   And seas resound his name from shore to shore;
   Ye tow'ring mountains sound his praise on high,
   In joyful notes ye verdant vales reply.

4 Ye monarchs of the earth, your Lord adore,
   To whom ye owe your delegated power;
   Ye judges, his impartial law revere;
   Be ev'ry sentence guided by his fear;
   Let senate, prince, and people join to raise
   The grateful tribute of obedient praise.

HYMN XXVII.

All Nature invoked to praise the Creator.

1 PRAISE the Lord, let praise employ
   In his courts your songs of joy;
   Let the spacious heavens around,
   Echo back the solemn sound.

2 Angels, your clear voices raise :
Him, ye heav'nly armies praise :
Sun and moon, with borrow'd light ;
All ye sparkling eyes of night ;

3 Vapours, lightning, hail and snow ;
Storms which, where he bids you, blow;
Waters, hanging in the air ;
Heav'n of heav'ns—his praise declare.

4 Let the earth his praise resound ;
Echoing rocks, and seas profound ;
Verdant vales, and mountains high ;
Cedars, tow'ring to the sky.

5 Princes, judges of the earth ;
All of high or humble birth ;
Youths and virgins, flourishing
In the beauty of your spring ;

6 All, whom life and breath inspire,
Come and join the grateful choir ;
Come, and all, with one accord,
Join to praise th' Almighty Lord.

HYMN XXVIII.

Thanks to God, our Preserver.

1 GREAT God ! to thee our grateful tongues
    United thanks shall raise :
Inspire our hearts to tune the songs
    Which celebrate thy praise.

2 From thine almighty forming hand
    We drew our vital pow'rs :
Our time revolves at thy command,
    In all its circling hours.

3 Thy pow'r, our ever prefent guard,
  From ev'ry ill defends;
While num'rous dangers hover round,
  Our help from thee defcends.

4 Beneath the fhadow of thy wings,
  How fweet is our repofe!
The morning-light renews the fprings
  From whence our comfort flows.

5 In celebration of thy praife
  We will employ our breath;
And, walking ftedfaft in thy ways,
  Will triumph over death.

HYMN XXIX.

God the Guide of his Servants.

1 HOW are thy fervants blefs'd, O Lord!
    How fure is their defence!
  Eternal Wifdom is their guide;
    Their help, Omnipotence.

2 In foreign realms, and lands remote,
    Supported by thy care;
  Through burning climes they pafs unhurt,
    And breathe in tainted air.

3 When by the dreadful tempeft borne,
    High on the broken wave,
  They know thou art not flow to hear,
    Nor impotent to fave.

4 The ftorm is laid, the winds retire,
    Obedient to thy will;
  The fea that roars at thy command,
    At thy command is ftill.

5 In midst of dangers, fears, and deaths,
  Thy goodness we'll adore,
And praise thee for thy mercies past,
  And humbly hope for more.

HYMN XXX.
Thanks for daily Protection.

1 GREAT God, how endless is thy love!
   Thy gifts are ev'ry ev'ning new;
  And morning mercies, from above,
  Gently distil, like early dew.

2 Thou spread'st the curtains of the night,
  Great Guardian of our sleeping hours!
  Thy sov'reign word restores the light,
  And quickens all our drowsy pow'rs.

3 We yield our pow'rs to thy command;
  To thee we consecrate our days;
  Perpetual blessings from thine hand
  Demand perpetual songs of praise.

HYMN XXXI.
Thanks for Mercies, temporal and spiritual.

1 LORD, when our raptur'd thought surveys
    Creation's beauties o'er,
  All nature joins to teach thy praise,
    And bid our souls adore.

2 The living tribes of countless forms,
    In earth, and sea, and air,
  The meanest flies, the smallest worms,
    Almighty pow'r declare.

3 Thy wisdom, power, and goodness, Lord,
In all thy works appear;
And, O! let man thy praise record,
Man, thy distinguish'd care!

4 From thee the breath of life he drew;
That breath thy pow'r maintains:
Thy tender mercy, ever new,
His brittle frame sustains.

5 Yet nobler favours claim his praise:
Of reason's light possess'd;
By revelation's brightest rays
Still more divinely bless'd.

6 Thy providence, his constant guard,
When threat'ning woes impend;
Or will th' impending dangers ward,
Or timely succours lend.

7 On us that providence has shone,
With gentle, smiling rays:
O let our lips and lives make known
Thy goodness and thy praise!

HYMN XXXII.
The Advantage of Divine Revelation.

1 WHEN Israel through the desert pass'd,
A fiery pillar went before,
To guide them through the dreary waste,
And lessen the fatigues they bore.

2 Such is the glorious word of God;
'Tis for our light and guidance given;
It sheds a lustre all abroad,
And points the path to bliss and heaven.

3 It fills the soul with sweet delight,
  And quickens its inactive powers;
  It sets our wandering footsteps right;
  Displays his love, and kindles ours.

4 Its promises rejoice the heart;
  Its doctrines are divinely true;
  Knowledge and pleasure it imparts;
  It comforts and instructs us too.

5 Ye favour'd lands, bless'd with this word;
  Ye saints, who feel its saving power;
  Unite your tongues to praise the Lord,
  And his distinguish'd grace adore.

HYMN XXXIII.
God our Shepherd.

1 OUR shepherd is the living Lord;
    Now shall our wants be well supply'd;
  His providence and holy word
  Become our safety and our guide.

2 In pastures where salvation grows,
  He makes us feed, he makes us rest;
  There living water gently flows,
  And all the food's divinely blest.

3 Our wand'ring feet his ways mistake;
  But he restores our soul to peace,
  And leads us, for his mercy's sake,
  In the fair paths of righteousness.

4 Amidst the darkness and the deeps,
  Thou art our comfort, thou our stay;
  Thy staff supports our feeble steps,
  Thy rod directs our doubtful way.

5 Though

5 Though we walk through the gloomy vale,
  Where death and all its terrors are,
  Our heart and hope shall never fail,
  For God our shepherd's with us there.

HYMN XXXIV.

✝ God our Shepherd.

1 THE Lord my shepherd is,
    I shall be well supply'd :
  Since he is mine, and I am his,
    What can I want beside ?

2 He leads me to the place,
    Where heav'nly pasture grows,
  Where living waters gently pass,
    And full salvation flows.

3 If e'er I go astray,
    He doth my soul reclaim,
  And guides me in his own right way,
    For his most holy name.

4 While he affords his aid,
    I cannot yield to fear :
  Tho' I should walk through death's dark shade,
    My shepherd's with me, there.

5 The bounties of thy love
    Shall crown my following days :
  Nor from thy house will I remove,
    Nor cease to speak thy praise.

HYMN XXXV.

God our Shepherd.

1 THE Lord my pasture shall prepare,
 And feed me with a shepherd's care;
 His presence shall my wants supply,
 And guard me with a watchful eye.

2 My noon-day walks he shall attend,
 And all my midnight hours defend:
 When in the sultry glebe I faint,
 Or on the thirsty mountains pant,

3 To fertile vales and dewy meads,
 My weary, wand'ring steps he leads,
 Where peaceful rivers, soft and slow,
 Amidst the verdant landskip flow.

4 Though in a bare and rugged way,
 Through devious lonely wilds I stray,
 Thy presence shall my pains beguile,
 The barren wilderness shall smile,

5 With sudden greens and herbage crown'd,
 And streams shall murmur all around.
 Though in the paths of death I tread,
 With gloomy horrors overspread,

6 My steadfast heart shall fear no ill,
 For thou, O Lord, art with me still:
 Thy friendly crook shall give me aid,
 And guide me through the dismal shade.

HYMN XXXVI.

God our Shepherd.

1 LO, my Shepherd's hand divine !
Want shall never more be mine;
In a pasture fair and large
He will feed his happy charge.

2 When I faint with summer's heat,
He will lead my weary feet
To the streams that, still and slow,
Thro' the verdant meadow flow.

3 He my soul anew will frame,
And his mercy to proclaim,
When thro' devious paths I stray,
Teach my steps the better way.

4 Thro' the dreary vale I tread,
By the shades of death o'erspread;
There I walk from terror free,
While protected, Lord, by thee.

HYMN XXXVII.

God our Shepherd.

1 THE Lord is my shepherd, my guardian, and guide;
Whatsoever I want, he will kindly provide;
To the sheep of his pasture his mercies abound,
His care and protection his flock will surround;
If e'er from his fold they should wander abroad,
His care will recall them, and fix their abode,
Where himself, in the midst, with a provident eye,
Will regard all their wants, and provide a supply.

2 The Lord is my shepherd, what then shall I fear?
What danger can frighten me while he is near?
Not when the time calls me to walk thro' the vale
Of the shadow of death, shall my heart ever fail;
Tho' afraid, of myself, to pursue the dark way,
Thy rod and thy staff be my comfort and stay;
For I know, by thy guidance, when once it is past,
To a fountain of life it will bring me at last.

3 The Lord is become my salvation and song,
His blessings shall follow me all my life long;
Whatsoever condition he places me in,
I am sure 'tis the best it could ever have been;
For the Lord he is good, and his mercies are sure;
He only afflicts us, in order to cure;
The Lord will I praise while I have any breath,
Be content all my life, and resign'd in my death.

HYMN XXXVIII.
God the Guide of the Humble.

1 WHOE'ER, with humble fear,
    To God his duty pays,
Shall find the Lord a faithful guide
    In all his righteous ways.

2 He those in virtue guides,
    Who his direction seek,
And in his sacred paths will lead
    The humble and the meek.

3 Thro' all the ways of God
    Both truth and mercy shine,
To those who, with religious hearts,
    To his bless'd will incline.

4 The meek the Lord will bless,
  And make them heirs of heaven;
True riches, with abundant peace,
  To humble souls are given.

HYMN XXXIX.

Creation and Providence.

1 YE humble souls, in God rejoice!
    Your Maker's praise becomes your voice,
  Great is your theme, your songs be new;
Sing of his name, his word, his ways,
His works of nature and of grace,
  How wise and holy, just and true!

2 Justice and truth he ever loves,
  And the whole earth his goodness proves,
    His word the heavenly arches spread;
How wide they shine from north to south!
And by the spirit of his mouth
    Were all the starry armies made.

3 He gathers the wide flowing seas,
  Those wat'ry treasures know their place
    In the vast storehouse of the deep:
He spake, and gave all nature birth;
And fires, and seas, and heav'n, and earth,
    His everlasting orders keep.

4 Ye that delight to serve the Lord,
  The honours of his name record,
    His sacred name forever bless;
Where'er the circling sun displays
His rising beams, or setting rays,
    Let ev'ry tongue his pow'r confess.

HYMN XL.
God hearing Prayer.

1 THRO' all the changing scenes of life,
   In trouble, and in joy,
The praises of my God shall still
   My heart and tongue employ.

2 Of his deliv'rance I will boast,
   Till all who are distress'd
From my example comfort take,
   And sooth their griefs to rest.

3 O magnify the Lord with me,
   With me exalt his name;
To him in my distress I cry'd,
   He to my rescue came.

4 With grateful hearts observe his ways,
   And on his goodness rest;
So will your own experience prove
   That pious souls are blest.

5 For while his fear inspires your breast,
   His mercy will be nigh,
To guard your lives from threat'ning ills,
   And all your wants supply.

HYMN XLI.
Providence and Grace.

1 HIGH in the heavens, eternal God,
   Thy goodness in full glory shines;
Thy truth shall break thro' ev'ry cloud
Which veils and darkens thy designs.

2 Forever firm thy justice stands,
 As mountains their foundations keep;
 Great are the wonders of thine hands,
 Thy judgments are a mighty deep!

3 Thy mercy makes the earth thy care,
 Thy providence is kind and large;
 Angels and men thy bounty share,
 The whole creation is thy charge.

4 Since of thy goodness all partake,
 With what assurance may the just
 Thy shelt'ring wings their refuge make,
 And saints to thy protection trust.

5 Such guests shall to thy courts be led,
 And there enjoy a rich repast,
 There drink, as from a fountain head,
 Of joys which shall forever last.

6 With thee the springs of life remain,
 Thy presence is eternal day;
 O let thy saints thy favour gain,
 To upright hearts thy truth display.

HYMN XLII.
Gratitude to God.

1 WHEN all thy mercies, O my God,
   My rising soul surveys,
 Transported with the view, I'm lost
   In wonder, love and praise!

2 O, how shall words with equal warmth
   The gratitude declare,
 That glows within my ravish'd heart?
   But thou canst read it there.

3 Thy providence my life sustain'd,
    And all my wants redrest,
When in the silent womb I lay,
    And hung upon the breast.

4 To all my weak complaints and cries
    Thy mercy lent an ear,
Ere yet my feeble thoughts had learnt
    To form themselves in pray'r.

5 Unnumber'd comforts to my soul
    Thy tender care bestow'd,
Before my infant heart conceiv'd
    From whom those comforts flow'd.

6 When in the slipp'ry paths of youth
    With heedless steps I ran,
Thine arm unseen convey'd me safe,
    And led me up to man.

7 Through hidden dangers, toils and deaths,
    It gently clear'd my way,
And through the pleasing snares of vice,
    More to be fear'd than they.

8 Ten thousand thousand precious gifts
    My daily thanks employ;
Nor is the least a cheerful heart,
    That tastes those gifts with joy.

9 Through every period of my life
    Thy goodness I'll pursue;
And after death, in distant worlds,
    The glorious theme renew.

10 When nature fails, and day and night
    Divide thy works no more;
My ever grateful heart, O Lord,
    Thy mercy shall adore.

11 Through all eternity, to thee
    A joyful song I'll raise;
For, oh! eternity's too short
    To utter all thy praise.

HYMN XLIII.
Thanksgiving for the Fruits of the Earth.

1 O PRAISE the Lord, our heav'nly King,
    Who makes the earth his care;
Visits the pastures ev'ry spring,
    And bids the grass appear.

2 The clouds, like rivers rais'd on high,
    Pour out, at his command,
Their wat'ry blessings from the sky,
    To cheer the thirsty land.

3 The soften'd ridges of the field
    Permit the corn to spring;
The vallies rich provision yield,
    And the glad labourers sing.

4 The little hills, on ev'ry side,
    Rejoice at falling show'rs;
The meadows, dress'd in all their pride,
    Perfume the air with flow'rs.

5 The barren clouds, refresh'd with rain,
    Promise a joyful crop;
The parched grounds look green again,
    And raise the reaper's hope.

6 The various months thy goodness crowns:
   How bounteous are thy ways!
 The bleating flocks spread o'er the downs,
   And shepherds shout thy praise.

7 Thine is the cheerful day, and thine
   The still returns of night;
 Thou hast prepar'd the glorious sun
   And ev'ry feebler light.

8 By thee the borders of the earth
   In perfect order stand;
 The summer's warmth and winter's cold
   Attend on thy command.

HYMN XLIV.

Thanksgiving for the Fruits of the Earth.

1 O THOU, who to our humble pray'r
   Dost always bend thy list'ning ear!
 To thee shall all mankind repair,
   And at thy gracious throne appear.

2 By wond'rous acts, O God, most just!
   Have we thy gracious answer found;
 In thee remotest nations trust,
   And those whom stormy waves surround.

3 From out thy unexhausted store
   Thy rain relieves the thirsty ground;
 Makes lands, that barren were before,
   With corn and richest fruits abound.

4 On rising ridges down it pours,
   And ev'ry furrow'd valley fills;
 Thou mak'st them soft with gentle show'rs,
   In which a blest increase distils.

Thy

5 Thy goodnefs does the circling year
      With frefh returns of plenty crown;
And where thy glorious paths appear,
      The fruitful clouds drop fatnefs down.

6 They drop on barren forefts, chang'd
      By them to paftures frefh and green;
The hills about, in order rang'd,
      In beauteous robes of joy are feen.

7 Large flocks, with fleecy wool, adorn
      The cheerful downs; the vallies bring
A plenteous crop of full-ear'd corn,
      And feem for joy to fhout and fing.

☩ HYMN XLV.
Thankſgiving for Deliverance from Danger at Sea.

1 LORD! for the juft thou doft provide;
      Thou art their fure defence:
Eternal Wifdom is their guide;
      Their help, Omnipotence.

2 Though they through foreign lands fhould roam
      And breathe the tainted air
In burning climates, far from home,
      Yet thou, their God, art there.

3 Thy goodnefs fweetens ev'ry foil,
      Makes ev'ry country pleafe;
Thou on the fnowy hills doft fmile,
      And fmooth'ft the rugged feas.

4 When waves on waves, to heav'n uprear'd,
      Defy'd the pilot's art;
When terror in each face appear'd,
      And forrow in each heart;

5 To thee I rais'd my humble pray'r
   To snatch me from the grave;
I found "thine ear not slow to hear,
  " Nor short thine arm to save."

6 Thou gav'st the word—the winds did cease,
   The storms obey'd thy will;
The raging sea was hush'd in peace,
   And ev'ry wave lay still.

7 For this, my life, in ev'ry state,
   A life of praise shall be;
And death (when death shall be my fate)
   Shall join my soul to thee.

HYMN XLVI.
A Funeral Thought.

1 HARK! from the tombs a doleful sound!
   My ears, attend the cry!
"Ye living men, come view the ground
" Where ye must shortly lie.

2 " Princes, this clay must be your bed,
  " In spite of all your pow'rs;
" The tall, the wise, and rev'rend head,
  " Must be as low as ours."

3 Great God! is this our certain doom?
   And are we still secure?
Still walking downwards to our tomb,
   And yet prepare no more?

4 Then teach us, Lord, th' uncertain sum
   Of our short days to mind;
That to true wisdom all our hearts
   May ever be inclin'd.

HYMN XLVII.
The Goodness of God.

1 BE thou exalted, O my God,
   Above the heav'ns where angels dwell;
   Thy pow'r on earth be known abroad,
   And land to land thy wonders tell.

2 My heart is fix'd; my tongue shall raise
   Immortal honours to thy name;
   Awake, my tongue, to sound his praise—
   My tongue, the glory of my frame.

3 In thee, my God, are all the springs
   Of boundless love, and grace unknown;
   All the rich blessings Nature brings
   Are gifts descending from thy throne.

4 High o'er the earth thy goodness reigns,
   And reaches to the utmost sky;
   Thy truth to endless years remains,
   When lower worlds dissolve and die.

5 Be thou exalted, O my God,
   Above the heav'ns, where angels dwell;
   Thy pow'r on earth be known abroad,
   And land to land thy wonders tell.

HYMN XLVIII.
The Pleasure and Advantage of Publick Worship.

1 GREAT God, attend, while Sion sings
   The joy that from thy presence springs:
   To spend one day with thee on earth
   Exceeds a thousand days of mirth.

2 God

2 God is our sun—he makes our day;
   God is our shield—he guards our way
   From all th' assaults of hell and sin,
   From foes without and foes within.

3 All needful grace will God bestow,
   And crown that grace with glory too;
   He gives us all things, and withholds
   No real good from upright souls.

4 Cheerful they walk, with growing strength,
   Till all shall meet in heav'n at length;
   Till all before thy face appear,
   And join in nobler worship there.

HYMN XLIX.
God our Protector.

1 HE who hath made his refuge God,
   Shall find a most secure abode,
   Shall walk all day beneath his shade,
   And safe at night shall rest his head.

2 He guides our feet, he guards our way;
   His morning smiles bless all the day;
   He spreads the ev'ning veil, and keeps
   The silent hours while Nature sleeps.

3 Then will I say, My God, thy pow'r
   Shall be my fortress and my tow'r;
   I, who am form'd of feeble dust,
   Make thine almighty arm my trust.

4 Up to the hills I lift mine eyes,
   Th' eternal hills beyond the skies;
   Thence all her help my soul derives,
   There my Almighty Refuge lives.

5 He lives, the everlasting God,
Who built the world, and spread the flood;
He lives, and by his heav'nly care
Preserves my life from ev'ry snare.

HYMN L.

God's Truth and Equity.

1 SING to the Lord a joyful song;
Earth to his praise the note prolong,
Till realms remote his acts have known,
And man's whole race his wonders own.

2 Great is the Lord, and great his praise!
What God, like him, our fear can raise?
Not such as heathen lands afford,
Created first, and then ador'd.

3 Exult, ye heav'ns! Exult, O earth!
And, partner in the sacred mirth,
Let ocean in its fulness rise,
And thunder to the distant skies!

4 Rich in his gifts, ye fields, rejoice!
While in his praise the woods their voice
Exalt, and hail, with lowly nod,
The presence of th' approaching God!

5 He comes, in awful pomp array'd!
He comes, to judge the world he made!
TRUTH shall with him the cause decide,
And EQUITY his sentence guide.

HYMN LI.
The Mercies of God.

1 AWAKE, my soul! Awake, my tongue!
My God demands the grateful song;
Let all my inmost pow'rs record
The wond'rous goodness of the Lord!

2 Divinely free his mercy flows,
Forgives my sins, allays my woes;
He bids approaching death remove,
And crowns me with a father's love.

3 My youth, decay'd, his pow'r repairs;
His hand sustains my growing years;
He satisfies my mouth with food,
And feeds my soul with heav'nly good.

4 His mercy with unchanging rays
Forever shines, though time decays;
And children's children shall record
The truth and goodness of the Lord.

5 While all his works his praise proclaim,
And men and angels bless his name,
O let my heart, my life, my tongue,
Attend, and join the sacred song!

HYMN LII.
God kind and merciful.

1 LET ev'ry tongue thy goodness speak,
Thou sov'reign Lord of all!
Thy strength'ning hands uphold the weak,
And raise the poor that fall.

2 When sorrow bows the spirit down,
    Or virtue lies distrest
Beneath some proud oppressor's frown,
    Thou giv'st the mourners rest.

3 Thy grace supports our tott'ring days,
    And guides our giddy youth:
Holy and just are all thy ways,
    And all thy words are truth.

4 Thou know'st the pains thy servants feel;
    Thou hear'st thy children's cry;
And, their best wishes to fulfil,
    Thy grace is ever nigh.

5 Thy mercy never shall remove
    From men of heart sincere,
To save the souls, whose humble love
    Is join'd with holy fear.

HYMN LIII.
Praise to God for his Goodness and Truth.

1 I'LL praise my Maker while I've breath,
    And when my voice is lost in death,
      Praise shall employ my nobler pow'rs;
My days of praise shall ne'er be past,
While life, and thought, and being last,
    Or immortality endures.

2 Happy the man whose hopes rely
    On Nature's God--he made the sky,
      And earth, and seas, with all their train:
His truth forever stands secure,
He saves th' opprest, he feeds the poor,
    And none shall find his promise vain.

3 The Lord hath eyes to give the blind,
　The Lord supports the sinking mind,
　　He sends the lab'ring conscience peace,
　He helps the stranger in distress,

　The widow and the fatherless,
　　And grants the prisoner sweet release.
4 I'll praise him while he lends me breath,
　And when my voice is lost in death,
　　Praise shall employ my nobler pow'rs;
　My days of praise shall ne'er be past,
　While life, and thought, and being last,
　　Or immortality endures.

HYMN LIV.
Thanks for the Gospel.

1 GOD, who in various methods told
　　His mind and will to saints of old,
　Sent his own son with truth and grace,
　To teach us in these latter days.

2 Our nation reads the written word,
　That book of life, that true record;
　The bright inheritance of heav'n
　Is by this sure conveyance giv'n.

3 God's kindest thoughts are here exprest,
　Able to make us wise and blest;
　The doctrines are divinely true,
　Fit for reproof and comfort too.

4 O render thanks to God above,
　For his rich grace, his boundless love;
　Let all mankind receive his word,
　And ev'ry nation praise the Lord.

HYMN LV.

The Blessings of the Gospel.

1 BEHOLD the morning sun
   Begins his glorious way;
His beams thro' all the nations run,
   And life and light convey.

2 But where the gospel comes
   It spreads diviner light;
It calls dead sinners from their tombs,
   And gives the blind their sight.

3 How perfect is thy word,
   And all thy judgments just,
Forever sure thy promise, Lord,
   Which we securely trust.

4 Thou gracious God, how plain
   Are thy directions giv'n!
O may we never read in vain,
   But find the path to heav'n.

5 While with our heart and tongue
   We spread thy praise abroad,
Accept the worship and the song,
   Our Father and our God!

HYMN LVI.

The Glory and Success of the Gospel.

1 THE heavens declare thy glory, Lord,
   In every star thy wisdom shines;
But, in the volume of thy word,
   We read thy name in fairer lines.

2 Sun, moon, and stars, convey thy praise
Round the whole earth, and never stand:
So, when thy truth began its race,
It touch'd and glanc'd on every land.

3 Nor let thy spreading gospel rest,
Till thro' the earth thy truth has run,
Till it has all the nations blest,
That see the light or feel the sun.

4 Great God of righteousness, arise,
Bless the dark world with heavenly light,
Thy gospel makes the simple wise,
Thy laws are pure, thy judgment right.

5 Thy noblest wonders here we view,
In souls renew'd and sins forgiven,
Lord, cleanse our sins, our souls renew,
And make thy word our guide to heaven.

HYMN LVII.

Praise to the God of our Salvation.

1 HAIL the God of our salvation,
    Triumph in redeeming love;
Let us with glad exultation
    Imitate the blest above.

2 Light of those whose dreary dwelling
    Border'd on the shades of death,
He hath by his grace revealing,
    Scatter'd all the clouds beneath.

3 Father thou art all compassion,
    Pure unbounded love thou art;
Hail the God of our salvation,
    Praise him ev'ry thankful heart.

4 Joyfully

4 Joyfully on earth adore him,
   Till in heaven we take our place,
There enraptur'd, fall before him,
   Lost in wonder, love and praise.

HYMN LVIII.
Rejoicing in the Hope of Glory.

1 THOU God of our salvation,
   We joyfully adore thee,
     Trusting thy care,
     To keep us here
And bring us safe to glory.

2 We lift our hearts and voices
With blest anticipation
     And shout aloud,
     And give to God
The praise of our salvation.

3 We lift our voice exulting
In thine almighty favour,
     The love divine
     Which made us thine
Shall keep us thine forever.

4 By faith we see the glory
To which thou wilt restore us,
     We lift our eyes
     To that high prize
Which thou hast set before us.

5 Thou God of our salvation
We joyfully adore thee;
     We trust thy care
     To keep us here
And bring us safe to glory.

✝ HYMN LIX.
Fruitful Showers, Emblems of the Gospel.

1 MARK the soft-falling snow,
    And the diffusive rain,
To heaven from whence it fell,
    It turns not back again,
But waters earth through every pore,
And calls forth all its secret store.

2 Array'd in living green,
    The hills and valleys shine,
And man and beast is fed
    By providence divine;
The harvest bows its golden ears,
The copious seed of future years.

3 "So saith the God of grace,
    "My gospel shall descend,
"Almighty to effect
    "The purpose I intend;
"Millions of souls shall feel its power,
"And bear it down to millions more.

4 "Joy shall begin their march,
    "And peace protect their ways.
"While all the mountains round
    "Echo melodious praise;
"The vocal groves shall sing THE GOD,
"And every tree consenting nod."

HYMN XL.
✝ *The Equity of the Divine Dispensations.*

1 FATHER of men, who can complain
    Under thy mild and equal reign?
Who does a weight of duty share
More than his aids and pow'rs can bear?

2 With diff'ring climes and diff'ring lands,
With fruitful plains and barren sands,
Thy hand hath form'd this earthly round,
And set each nation in its bound.

3 With like variety thy ray
Here sheds a full, there fainter day,
While all are in their measure show'd
The way to happiness and God.

4 O the unbounding grace which brought
To us the words by Jesus taught!
So blest and with such hopes inspir'd,
How much is giv'n, how much requir'd!

HYMN LXI.
Christ's Resurrection a Pledge of ours.

1 BLESS'D be the everlasting God,
   The Father of our Lord!
Be his abounding mercy prais'd,
   His majesty ador'd!

2 When from the dead he rais'd his son,
   And call'd him to the sky,
He gave our souls a lively hope,
   That they should never die.

3 What tho' thy uncontroul'd decree
   Command us back to dust?
Yet, as the Lord our Saviour rose,
   So all his followers must.

4 There's an inheritance divine
   Reserv'd against that day;
'Tis uncorrupted, undefil'd,
   And cannot fade away.

5 We by thy pow'r, O God, are kept,
   Till the salvation come;
We walk by faith, as strangers here,
   'Till thou shalt call us home.

✝ HYMN LXII.

Thanks to God for Blessings in Christ.

1   LOUD be thy name ador'd,
     Thy titles spread abroad,
  Of Christ our glorious Lord,
     The Father and the God;
Thro' such a Son thy church's head,
O'er worlds unknown thine honours spread.

2   Ten thousand gifts of love
     From thee thro' him descend,
  And bear our souls above,
     To joys that never end;
Sustain'd by God, to heaven they soar
And thro' the road his arm adore.

3   Ten thousand songs of praise
     Shall for thy mercies rise,
  And, thro' eternal days,
     Shall echo round the skies;
New shouts we'll give, and loud proclaim
The glories of thy sacred name.

✝ HYMN LXIII.
The Spring an Emblem of Gospel Blessings.

1 PRAISE God, from whom all blessings flow,
   Whose goodness crowns the varied year;
While nature's works his bounty show,
Let gratitude salute him here;
   Swell, gently swell, the solemn song,
   Now pour the bounding notes along,
Teach choirs below, to choirs above,
To echo back the common lay,
And, as they praise unbounded love,
To join in bounty's holiday.
      To God the universal King
      Be sacred every grateful choir!
      In ceaseless hymns, all praises sing,
      That endless bounty can inspire!

2 All lost, beneath stern winter's reign,
Creation's genial powers appear'd,
Spring call'd them into life again,
See, budding verdure shews they heard;
   Bless, bless, O man! the kind design,
   Whose nobler counter-part is thine!
Thy powers a gloomier winter froze,
Till thy Messiah's cheering ray,
Prolifick of fair truth, arose,
And shed the blaze of mental day.
      To God the universal King
      Be sacred every grateful choir!
      In ceaseless hymns, all praises sing,
      That endless bounty can inspire!

3 All spotless, as the truth he taught,
Free, as the mercy he display'd,
He shew'd what human duty ought,
He did what heavenly goodness bade;
   Enforc'd each just command he gave,
   Nor liv'd, nor dy'd, in vain to save.

Praise God, whose heavenly mercy sent
His Son to save a sinful race,
Let ev'ry heart with one consent
Adore the free, the wond'rous grace.
    To God the universal King,
    Be sacred every grateful choir!
    In ceaseless hymns all praises sing,
    That endless mercy can inspire!

HYMN LXIV.
The Invitation of the Gospel.

1 LET every mortal ear attend,
    And every heart rejoice:
The trumpet of the gospel sounds
    With an inviting voice.

2 Ho! all ye weary wand'ring souls
    That feed upon the wind,
And vainly strive with earthly toys
    To fill an empty mind.

3 Eternal wisdom has prepar'd
    A soul-reviving feast,
And bids your longing appetites
    The rich provision taste.

4 Ho! ye that pant for living streams,
    And pine away and die;
Here you may quench your raging thirst
    With streams that never dry.

5 Rivers of love and mercy here
    In a rich ocean join;
Salvation in abundance flows
    Like floods of milk and wine.

6 The happy gates of gospel grace
   Stand open night and day :
Lord, we are come to seek supplies,
   And drive our wants away.

HYMN LXV.

God exalted above all Praise.

1 ALMIGHTY Author of our frame,
   To thee our vital pow'rs belong ;
Thy praise (delightful, glorious theme !)
Demands our heart, our life, our tongue.

2 Our hearts, our lives, our tongues, are thine :
   O be thy praise their best employ !
But may our songs with angels join,
   Nor sacred awe forbid the joy !

3 Thy glories the seraphick lyre,
   On all its strings, attempts in vain :
Then how shall mortals dare aspire,
   In thought, to try th' unequal strain ?

4 Yet the great Sov'reign of the skies
   To mortals bends a gracious ear ;
Nor the mean tribute will despise,
   When offer'd with a heart sincere.

5 Great God, accept the humble praise,
   And guide our heart, and guide our tongue,
While to thy name we trembling raise
   The grateful, though unworthy, song.

HYMN LXVI.
God exalted above all Praise.

1 BEFORE the awful throne we bow
  Of heav'n's Eternal King;
To him present the solemn vow,
  And hymns of praises sing.

2 How weak, great God, our noblest songs
  To magnify thy ways!
Nor human nor angelick tongues
  Can shew forth all thy praise.

3 Yet be it now our chief delight
  Our feeble notes to join,
Until with angels we unite
  In anthems more divine.

4 Nor from thy presence cast away
  The off'ring that we bring:
Lord! teach our hearts aright to pray,
  And tune our lips to sing.

HYMN LXVII.
Praise to the great and good God.

1 LONG as we live, we'll bless thy name,
  Great King, and God of love!
Our work and joy shall be the same
  In the bright world above.

2 Thy grace shall dwell upon our tongues;
  And, while our lips rejoice,
The men, who hear our sacred songs,
  Shall join their cheerful voice.

3 Fathers to sons shall teach thy name,
 And children learn thy ways;
Ages to come thy truth proclaim,
 And nations sound thy praise.

4 Thy glorious deeds, of ancient date,
 Shall thro' the world be known;
Thine arm of pow'r, thy heav'nly state,
 With publick splendour shown.

5 The world is govern'd by thy hands,
 The people rul'd by love;
And thine eternal kingdom stands,
 Though rocks and hills remove.

HYMN LXVIII.
Invocation to praise God.

1 YE tribes of earth, in God rejoice;
 His presence hail, with thankful voice;
To him your willing homage pay,
And wake the tributary lay;
Submissive to his will, in him
Behold the God of Gods supreme.

2 With conscious wonder oft survey'd,
He, not ourselves, our frame has made;
The subjects of his pow'r we stand,
The sheep that own his guiding hand:
O enter then his gates with praise,
To him your loudest accents raise.

3 With grateful hearts his love proclaim,
And bless, O bless his awful name;
For truth in him, and mercy, live;
That truth shall time itself survive;
That mercy, thro' the length of days,
Unclouded, pour its healing rays.

HYMN LXIX.

Praise and Thanksgiving.

1 OUR Maker, and our King,
   To thee our all we owe,
Thy sovereign bounty is the spring
   From whence our blessings flow.

2 Thou ever good and kind,
   A thousand reasons move,
A thousand obligations bind,
   Our hearts to grateful love.

3 The creatures of thy hand,
   On thee alone we live;
Great God, thy benefits demand
   More praise than life can give.

4 O let thy grace inspire
   Our souls with strength divine;
Let all our powers to thee aspire,
   And all our days be thine.

HYMN LXX.

Praise and Thanksgiving.

1 HOLY, holy, holy Lord!
   Be thy glorious name ador'd!
Lord, thy mercies never fail;
Hail, celestial goodness, hail!

2 Tho' unworthy, Lord, thine ear,
Our humble hallelujahs hear:
Purer praise we hope to bring,
When around thy throne we sing.

3 While on earth ordain'd to stay,
  Guide our footsteps in thy way,
  Till we come to reign with thee,
  And all thy glorious greatness see.

4 Then no tongue shall silent be,
  And all shall join in harmony;
  That, thro' heav'n's all-spacious round,
  Thy praise, O God, may ever sound.

5 Lord, thy mercies never fail:
  Hail, celestial goodness, hail!
  Holy, holy, holy Lord,
  Be thy glorious name ador'd!

HYMN LXXI.
Praise and Thanksgiving.

1 HAIL, thou eternal King!
  Thy ceaseless praise we sing:
  Praise shall our glad tongues employ,
  Praise o'erflow our grateful soul,
  While we vital breath enjoy,
  While eternal ages roll.

2 Let earth's remotest bound
  With thy glad praise resound!
  From thine high and holy place,
  Where thou dost in glory reign,
  Thou, in condescending grace,
  Deign'st to view the sons of men.

3 O Lord, thou God of love!
  While we thy mercy prove,
  Praise shall our glad tongues employ,
  Praise o'erflow our grateful soul,
  While we vital breath enjoy,
  While eternal ages roll.

HYMN LXXII.

Praise and Thanksgiving.

1 SOV'REIGN Lord of might and glory!
   Author of our mortal frame!
Joyfully we bow before thee,
   And extol thine holy name:
      Hallelujah!
   Ever sacred be the theme!

2 Kind Dispenser of each blessing,
   Which surrounds the human race!
May we, gratefully possessing,
   Still adore thy boundless grace:
      Hallelujah!
   Praise to God, immortal praise!

3 While with joyful exultation
   We attend before thy throne,
Let us, with glad acclamation,
   Thine abundant mercies own:
      Hallelujah!
   Praise belongs to thee alone!

4 In thine ev'ry dispensation,
   Grace and mercy we descry;
Thou, the God of our salvation,
   To preserve us, still art nigh:
      Hallelujah!
   Glory be to God on high!

HYMN LXXIII.

Praise and Thanksgiving.

1 O Come let us join,
   With musick divine,
   Our Creator to praise,
And joyfully sing his unspeakable grace!
   Thou light of mankind,
   Shine into each mind,
   And clearly reveal
Thy perfect and good and acceptable will.

2 Our heavenly guide
   With us will abide,
   His comfort impart,
And set up his kingdom of love in our heart;
   The heart that believes,
   His mercy receives,
   He will give us to prove,
His utmost salvation, his fulness of love.

HYMN LXXIV.

✠ *Doxology.*

1 FROM all who dwell below the skies,
   Let the Creator's praise arise;
Let the Almighty's name be sung,
Thro' ev'ry land, by ev'ry tongue.

2 Eternal are thy mercies, Lord,
  Eternal truth attends thy word;
Thy praise shall sound from shore to shore,
Till suns shall rise and set no more.

HYMN LXXV.
Humble Adoration.

1 LO God is here! let us adore,
 And humbly bow before his face,
Let all within us feel his power,
 Let all within us seek his grace;
Who know his power, his grace who prove,
Serve him with awe, with reverence love.

2 Being of beings, may our praise
 Thy courts with grateful fragrance fill,
Still may we stand before thy face,
 Still hear and do thy sovereign will;
To thee may all our thoughts arise
An acceptable sacrifice.

3 In thee we move, all things of thee
 Are full, thou source and life of all,
Thou vast unfathomable sea,
 On thee the God of love we call,
Thou art the God, thou art the Lord,
Be thou by all thy works ador'd.

† HYMN LXXVI.
God the Father of our Spirits.

1 ETERNAL Source of life and thought!
 Be all beneath thyself forgot,
While thee great Parent Mind we own,
In prostrate homage round thy throne.

2 While in themselves our souls survey
 Of thee some faint reflected ray,
They, wond'ring, to their Father rise:
His pow'r, how vast! his thoughts, how wise!

3 O may

3 O may we live before thy face
  Th' obedient children of thy grace,
  And thro' each path of duty move
  With filial awe and filial love.

4 Call us away from flesh and sense;
  Thy sov'reign hand can draw us thence;
  We would obey the voice divine,
  And all inferior joys resign.

HYMN LXXVII.

For the Lord's Day.

1 GREAT God, this sacred day of thine
  Demands our souls collected powers!
  May we employ in work divine
  These solemn, these devoted hours!
  O may our souls adoring own
  The grace which calls us to thy throne!

2 The word of life dispens'd to day,
  Invites us to a heavenly feast;
  May every ear the call obey,
  Be every heart a humble guest!
  Let all draw near, and tasting prove
  The sweetness of thy boundless love.

3 Thy truth's most pow'rful aid impart;
  O may thy word, with life divine,
  Engage the ear, and warm the heart!
  Then shall the day indeed be thine;
  Then shall our souls adoring own
  The grace which calls us to thy throne.

HYMN LXXVIII.

For the Lord's Day.

1 OUR hearts shall triumph in the Lord,
   And bless his works, and bless his word;
His works of grace! how bright they shine!
How deep his counsels! how divine!

2 So shall we share a glorious part,
When grace hath well refin'd our heart,
And fresh supplies of joy are shed,
Like holy oil to cheer our head.

3 Then shall we see, and hear, and know,
All we desir'd or wish'd below;
And every power find sweet employ
In that eternal world of joy.

HYMN LXXIX.

The divine Blessing implored.

1 AUTHOR of Good, to thee we come;
   Thy ever wakeful eye
Alone can all our wants discern,
   Thy hand alone supply.

2 O let thy fear within us dwell,
   Thy love our footsteps guide:
That love shall vainer loves expel;
   That fear, all fears beside.

3 And since, by error's force subdu'd,
   Too oft the stubborn will
Mistaken shuns the latent good,
   And grasps the specious ill;

4 Not to our wish, but to our want,
   Do thou thy gifts apply;
Unask'd, what good thou knowest, grant;
   What ill, tho' ask'd, deny.

HYMN LXXX.

Divine Guidance implored.

1 O That the Lord would guide our ways
   To keep his statutes still!
O that the Lord would grant us grace
   To know and do his will!

2 Since we are strangers here below,
   Let not thy path be hid;
But mark the road our feet should go,
   And be our constant guide.

3 Order our footsteps by thy word,
   And make our hearts sincere;
Let sin have no dominion, Lord,
   But keep our conscience clear.

4 Make us to walk in wisdom's way,
   'Tis a delightful road;
It leads to realms of endless day,
   It leads to thine abode.

HYMN LXXXI.

Imploring divine Direction.

1 LORD, through the dubious paths of life,
   Thy feeble servant guide;
Supported by thy powerful arm,
   My footsteps shall not slide.

2 To thee, O my unerring guide!
   I would myself resign;
In all my ways acknowledge thee,
   And form my will by thine.

3 Thus shall each blessing of thine hand
   Be doubly sweet to me;
And in new griefs I still shall have
   A refuge, Lord, in thee.

4 Lord, by thy counsel whilst I live,
   Guide thou my wand'ring feet;
And when my course on earth is run,
   Conduct me to thy feat.

HYMN LXXXII.

The divine Protection and Blessing implored.

1 THY presence, everlasting God,
   Wide o'er all nature spreads abroad;
Thy watchful eyes, which cannot sleep,
In ev'ry place thy children keep.

2 While near each other we remain,
   Thou dost our lives and souls sustain;
When absent, happy if we share
Thy smiles, thy counsels, and thy care.

3 To thee we all our ways commit,
And seek our comforts near thy seat;
Still on our souls vouchsafe to shine,
And guard and guide us still as thine.

4 Give us, in thy beloved house,
Again to pay our thankful vows;
Or, if that joy no more be known,
Give us to meet around thy throne.

HYMN LXXXIII.

The divine Blessing besought on our lawful Employments.

1 SHINE on our souls, eternal God!
  With rays of glory shine!
O let thy favour crown our days,
  And all their round be thine!

2 Did we not raise our hearts to thee,
  Our hands might toil in vain;
Small joy success itself would give,
  If thou thy love restrain.

3 With thee let ev'ry week begin,
  With thee each day be spent,
For thee each fleeting hour improv'd,
  Since each by thee is lent.

4 Midst hourly cares, may love present
  Its incense to thy throne;
And while the world our hands employs,
  Our hearts be thine alone.

HYMNS LXXXIV. LXXXV.

HYMN LXXXIV.
Growth in Grace desired.

1 PRAISE to thy name, eternal God!
  For all the grace thou shed'st abroad,
For all thy influence from above,
To warm our souls with sacred love.

2 Bless'd be thy hand, which from the skies
Brought down this plant of paradise,
And gave its heav'nly beauties birth
To deck this wilderness of earth.

3 Unchanging Sun! thy beams display,
To drive the frost and storms away;
Make all thy potent virtues known,
To cheer a plant so much thy own.

4 May thy blest spirit deign to blow
Fresh gales of heav'n on shrubs below;
So shall they grow, and breathe abroad
A fragrance grateful to our God.

HYMN LXXXV.
Sanctifying Grace implored.

1 FOUNTAIN of being! God of love!
    To thee our hearts we raise;
Thine all-sustaining power we prove,
    And gladly sing thy praise.

2 Thine, wholly thine, we long to be;
    Our sacrifice receive;
Made, and preserv'd, and sav'd by thee,
    To thee ourselves we give.

3 Heavenward our every wish aspires;
   For all thy mercies store,
The sole return thy love requires,
   Is, that we ask for more.

4 For more we ask; we open, Lord,
   Our hearts t'embrace thy will;
Renew us by thy heav'nly grace,
   And with thy fulness fill.

5 Still may we find thy heavenly love
   Shed in our hearts abroad;
So shall we ever live, and move,
   And be with Christ in God.

HYMN LXXXVI.
Confidence in God our Father.

1 O GOD! on thee we all depend,
   On thy paternal care;
Thou wilt the father and the friend
   In every act appear.

2 With open hand and liberal heart
   Thou wilt our wants supply;
Thy heav'nly blessings still impart,
   And no good thing deny.

3 Our father knows what's good and fit,
   And wisdom guides his love;
To thine appointments we submit,
   And ev'ry choice approve.

4 In thy paternal love and care
   With cheerful hearts we trust;
Thy tender mercies boundless are,
   And all thy ways are just.

5 We cannot want, while God provides
    What he ordains is best;
And Heav'n, whate'er we want besides,
    Will give eternal rest.

HYMN LXXXVII.
The Presence of God our sure Support.

1 AND art thou with us, gracious Lord,
    To dissipate our fear?
Dost thou proclaim thyself our God,
    Our God forever near?

2 Doth thy right hand, which form'd the earth,
    And bears up all the skies,
Stretch from on high its friendly aid,
    When dangers round us rise?

3 On this support our souls shall lean,
    And banish every care;
The gloomy vale of death shall smile,
    If God be with us there.

4 While we thy gracious succour prove
    'Midst all our various ways,
The darkest shades through which we pass
    Shall echo with thy praise.

HYMN LXXXVIII.
Trust in God through all the Changes of Life.

1 FATHER of mercies, God of love,
    My father and my God,
I'll sing the honours of thy name,
    And spread thy praise abroad.

2 My soul, in pleasing wonder lost,
   Thy various love surveys;
 Where shall my grateful lips begin,
   Or where conclude thy praise?

3 In every period of my life
   Thy thoughts of love appear;
 Thy mercies gild each transient scene,
   And crown each passing year.

4 In all these mercies may my soul
   A father's bounty see,
 Nor let the gifts thy grace bestows
   Estrange my heart from thee.

5 Teach me, in time of deep distress,
   To own thy hand, my God;
 And in submissive silence hear
   The lessons of thy rod.

6 In every varying mortal state,
   Each bright, each gloomy scene,
 Give me a meek and humble mind,
   Still equal and serene.

7 Then will I close my eyes in death
   Without one anxious fear;
 For death itself is life, O God,
   If thou art with me there.

HYMN LXXXIX.
Reliance on Divine Protection.

1 ON thee, O God! we still depend,
   Our father and our constant friend;
 All that is good thou can'st supply,
 And put all threat'ning evil by.

2 Should

Should wars on ev'ry fide invade,
We'll fhelter feek beneath thy fhade;
We'll truft to thy paternal care,
Nor want, nor harm, nor danger fear.

We'll ftill refer ourfelves to thee,
And with our lot contented be;
With one confenting heart and voice,
Approve our heav'nly father's choice.

From earth we'll turn our longing eyes,
To regions far beyond the fkies;
O fit us for that bleft abode,
Where dwells our Father and our God.

HYMN XC. *Beautiful*
† *God the Support of frail Man.*

LORD, we adore thy wond'rous name,
    And make that name our truft,
Which rais'd at firft this curious frame,
    From mean and lifelefs duft.

A while thefe frail machines endure,
    The fabrick of a day;
Then know their vital pow'rs no more,
    But moulder back to clay.

Yet, Lord, whate'er is felt or fear'd,
    This thought is our repofe—
That he by whom this frame is rear'd,
    Its various weaknefs knows.

Thou view'ft us with a pitying eye,
    Whilft ftruggling with our load;
In pains and dangers thou art nigh,
    Our Father and our God.

5 Gently supported by thy love,
   We tend to realms of peace;
Where ev'ry pain shall far remove,
   And ev'ry frailty cease.

HYMN XCI.
† *God our Safety in Danger.*

1 HAPPY the souls who trust in God;
   They find a most secure abode;
They walk all day beneath his shade,
And there at night they rest their head.

2 If burning beams of noon conspire
To dart a pestilential fire,
God is their life, his wings are spread
To shield them with a healthful shade.

3 If vapours, with malignant breath,
Rise thick, and scatter midnight death,
The saints are safe; the poison'd air
Grows pure; for God himself is there.

HYMN XCII.
† *Trust in God under Troubles.*

1 SINCE thou, the everlasting God,
   Our father art become,
Our teacher, guardian, and our friend,
   And heav'n our final home;

2 We welcome all thy sov'reign will,
   For all that will is love;
And, when we know not what thou dost,
   We wait the light above.

3 Thy

3 Thy mercy, in the darkest gloom,
   Shall heav'nly rays impart;
And, when our eyelids close in death,
   Shall warm our trembling heart.

HYMN XCIII.

God the Strength of his People.

1 AWAKE, our souls! away, our fears!
   Let ev'ry trembling thought be gone!
Awake and run the heav'nly race,
And put a cheerful courage on!

2 True, 'tis a strait and thorny road,
   And mortal spirits tire and faint;
But they forget the mighty God,
That feeds the strength of every saint:

3 The mighty God, whose matchless pow'r,
   Is ever new and ever young;
And firm endures, while endless years
   Their everlasting circles run.

4 From him, the overflowing spring,
   Our souls shall draw a large supply;
While such as seek refreshing draughts
From mortal streams, shall droop and die.

5 Swift as an eagle cuts the air,
   We'll mount aloft to his abode;
On wings of love our souls shall fly,
Nor tire amidst the heavenly road.

HYMN XCIV.

Dependence and Resignation.

1 GREAT Lord of earth, and seas and skies!
 Thy wealth the needy world supplies;
 On thee alone the whole depends,
 Thy care to ev'ry part extends.

2 To thee perpetual thanks we owe,
 For all our comforts here below;
 Our daily bread thy bounty gives,
 And ev'ry rising want relieves.

3 The wastes of life thy pow'r repairs,
 Thy mercy stills tempestuous cares,
 And safe beneath thy guardian arm
 We live secur'd from ev'ry harm.

4 To thee we cheerful homage bring,
 In grateful hymns thy praises sing,
 Direct to thee our waiting eyes,
 And humbly look for fresh supplies.

5 We still are indigent and poor,
 Indebted much, yet lacking more;
 On thee we ever will depend,
 The rich, the sure, the faithful friend.

6 And, should thy measures seem severe,
 Calmly may we thy chast'ning bear,
 Without complaint, to thee submit,
 Th' unerring Judge of what is fit.

HYMN XCV.

Submission to the all-wise Decrees.

1 LORD, how mysterious are thy ways!
How blind are we! how mean our praise!
Thy steps can mortal eyes explore?
'Tis ours to wonder and adore!

2 Thy deep decrees from creature sight
Are hid in shades of awful night;
Amid the lines, with curious eye,
Not angel minds presume to pry.

3 Great God! I would not ask to see
What in futurity shall be;
If light and bliss attend my days,
Then let my future hours be praise.

4 Is darkness and distress my share,
Then let me trust thy guardian care;
Enough for me, if love divine
At length through every cloud shall shine.

5 Yet this my soul desires to know,
Be this my only wish below,
" That I am thine!"—This great request
Grant, bounteous God,—and I am blest!

HYMN XCVI.

Submission under Affliction.

1 THY people, Lord, have ever found
'Tis good to bear thy rod;
Afflictions make us learn thy law,
And live upon our God.

2 This is the comfort we enjoy;
   When new distress begins,
We read thy word, we run thy way,
   And hate our former sins.

3 Thy judgments, Lord, are always right,
   Though they may seem severe;
The sharpest sufferings we endure
   Flow from thy faithful care.

4 Before we knew thy chastening rod,
   Our feet were apt to stray;
Now may we learn to keep thy word,
   Nor wander from thy way.

HYMN XCVII.
Trust in God under Trouble.

1 COMMIT thou all thy ways
   And griefs into his hands,
To his sure truth and tender care
   Who heav'n and earth commands.

2 Who points the clouds their course,
   Whom winds and seas obey,
He shall direct thy wand'ring feet,
   He shall prepare thy way.

3 No profit canst thou gain
   By self-consuming care,
To him commend thy cause, his ear
   Attends the softest prayer.

4 Give to the winds thy fears,
   Hope and be undismay'd;
God hears thy sighs and counts thy tears,
   He will lift up thy head.

5 Through waves and clouds and storms
 He'll gently clear thy way;
Wait thou his time, so shall this night
 Soon end in joyous day.

6 Leave to his sovereign sway
 To choose and to command,
So shalt thou, grateful, own his way
 Is wise, and strong his hand.

† HYMN XCVIII. *Beautiful*
Weeping Seed-time, joyful Harvest.

1 THE darken'd sky, how thick it lowers!
 Troubled with storms, and big with showers;
No cheerful gleam of light appears,
But nature pours forth all her tears.

2 Yet let the sons of grace revive,
God bids the soul that seeks him live;
And from the gloomiest shade of night
Calls forth a morning of delight.

3 The seeds of extacy unknown,
Are in these water'd furrows sown;
See the green blades how thick they rise,
And with fresh verdure bless our eyes.

4 In secret foldings they contain
Unnumber'd ears of golden grain;
And heav'n shall pour its beams around,
'Till the ripe harvest load the ground.

5 Then shall the trembling mourner come,
And find his sheaves, and bear them home;
The voice long broke with sighs shall sing,
'Till heav'n with *Hallelujahs* ring.

HYMN

HYMN XCIX.
Wait on the Lord.

1 WAIT on the Lord, ye heirs of hope,
And let his word support your souls,
Well can he bear your courage up,
And all your foes and fears controul.

2 He waits his own well-chosen hour
Th' intended mercy to display,
And his paternal bowels move
While wisdom dictates the delay.

3 With mingled majesty and love,
At length he rises from his throne;
And while salvation he commands,
He makes his people's joy his own.

4 Blest are the humble souls that wait
With sweet submission to his will;
Harmonious all their passions move,
And in the midst of storms are still.

5 Still, till their Father's well-known voice
Wakens their silence into songs;
Then earth grows vocal with his praise,
And heav'n the grateful shout prolongs.

HYMN C.
Trusting in him who careth for us.

1 HOW gentle God's commands!
How kind his precepts are!
"Come, cast your burdens on the Lord,
And trust his constant care."

While providence supports,
  Let saints securely dwell;
That hand, which bears all nature up,
  Shall guide his children well.

Then let no anxious load
  Press down your weary mind;
Haste to your heav'nly Father's throne,
  And sweet refreshment find.

His goodness stands approv'd
  Down to the present day;
Then drop your burdens at his feet,
  And bear a song away.

HYMN CI.
God the Comfort of the pious Poor.

PRAISE to the Sov'reign of the sky,
  Who from his lofty throne
Looks down on all that humble lie,
  And calls such souls his own.

The haughty sinner he disdains,
  Tho' gems his temples crown;
And from the seat of pomp and pride,
  His vengeance hurls him down.

On his afflicted pious poor
  He makes his face to shine;
He fills their cottages of clay
  With lustre all divine.

Among the meanest of thy flock
  There let my dwelling be,
Rather than under gilded roofs,
  If absent, Lord, from thee.

HYMN

HYMN CII.
A living and dead Faith compared.

1 MISTAKEN souls! who dream of heaven,
  And make their empty boast
Of inward joys and sins forgiven,
  While they are slaves to lust.

2 The faith, which purifies the heart,
  The faith, which works by love,
Which bids our sinful joys depart,
  And lifts our thoughts above;

3 The faith, which conquers earth and hell
  By a celestial power;
This is the grace which shall prevail
  In the decisive hour.

HYMN CIII.
The Christian Warfare.

1 AWAKE my soul, lift up thine eyes;
  See where thy foes against thee rise,
In long array, a numerous host;
Awake my soul, or thou art lost.

2 See where rebellious passions rage,
And fierce desires and lusts engage;
The meanest foe of all the train
Has thousands and ten thousands slain.

3 Thou tread'st upon enchanted ground,
Perils and snares beset thee round;
Beware of all, guard every part,
But most the traitor in thy heart.

4 Come then, my soul, now learn to wield
The weight of thine immortal shield;
Put on the armour from above
Of heavenly truth and heavenly love.

5 The terror and the charm repel;
And powers of earth, and powers of hell;
The Man of Calv'ry triumph'd here;
Why should his faithful followers fear?

HYMN CIV.
The Christian's Resolution.

1 AH wretched souls, who still remain
Slaves to the world, and slaves to sin!
A nobler toil may we sustain,
A nobler satisfaction win.

2 May we resolve with all our heart,
With all our powers to serve the Lord;
Nor from his precepts e'er depart,
Whose service is a rich reward.

3 O be his service all our joy,
Around let our example shine,
Till others love the blest employ,
And join in labours so divine.

4 Be this the purpose of our soul,
Our solemn, our determin'd choice,
To yield to his supreme controul,
And in his kind commands rejoice.

5 O may we never faint nor tire,
Nor wandering leave his sacred ways;
Great God, accept our soul's desire,
And give us strength to love thy praise.

HYMN CV.
The Christian Race.

1 AWAKE, my soul, stretch ev'ry nerve,
    And press with vigour on;
An heavenly race demands thy zeal,
    And an immortal crown.

2 A cloud of witnesses around
    Hold thee in full survey;
Forget the steps already trod,
    And onward urge thy way.

3 'Tis God's all-animating voice
    Which calls thee from on high;
'Tis his own hand presents the prize
    To thine aspiring eye.

4 My soul, with sacred ardour fir'd,
    The glorious prize pursue;
And meet with joy the high command
    To bid this earth adieu.

HYMN CVI.
Holiness essential to a Christian Character.

1 SO let our lips and lives express
    The holy gospel we profess;
So let our works and virtues shine,
To prove the doctrine all divine.

2 Then shall we best proclaim abroad
The honours of our Saviour God,
When the salvation reigns within,
And grace subdues the power of sin.

3 Our flesh and sense must be deny'd,
Passion and envy, lust and pride;
While justice, temperance, truth and love,
Our inward piety approve.

4 Religion bears our spirits up,
While we expect that blessed hope,
The bright appearance of our LORD,
And faith stands leaning on his word.

HYMN CVII.

Holiness a necessary Qualification for Heaven.

1 NOR eye hath seen, nor ear hath heard,
Nor sense, nor reason known,
What joys the Father hath prepar'd,
For those who love the Son.

2 But the good Spirit of the Lord
Reveals a heav'n to come;
The beams of glory, in the word,
Allure and guide us home.

3 Pure are the joys above the sky,
And all the region peace;
No wanton tongue, nor envious eye,
Can see or taste the bliss.

HYMN CVIII.
Blessed are the Poor in Spirit.

1 YE humble souls complain no more,
    Let faith survey your future store,
How happy, how divinely blest,
The sacred words of truth attest.

2 When conscious grief laments sincere,
    And pours the penitential tear;
Hope points to your dejected eyes
A bright reversion in the skies:

3 A kingdom of immense delight,
Where health, and peace, and joy unite,
Where undeclining pleasures rise,
And every wish hath full supplies:

4 A kingdom which can ne'er decay,
Tho' time sweeps earthly thrones away:
The state, which power and truth sustain,
Unmov'd forever must remain.

5 Great God, to thee we breathe our prayer;
If thou confirm our interest there,
Enroll'd among thy happy poor,
Our largest wishes ask no more.

HYMN CIX.
The Happiness of a real Christian.

1 HOW happy is the Christian's state!
    His sins are all forgiven,
A cheering ray confirms the grace,
    And lifts his soul to heaven.

2 Though

2 Though in a rugged path of life
    He heaves the pensive sigh,
  Yet, trusting in his God, he finds
    Delivering grace is nigh.

3 If to prevent his wandering steps
    He feels the chastening rod,
  The gentle stroke shall bring him back
    To his forgiving God.

HYMN CX.
The hidden Life of a Christian.

1 O Happy souls, who live on high!
    While men lie groveling here,
  Their hopes are fix'd above the sky,
    And faith forbids their fear.

2 Their conscience knows no secret stings,
    While grace and joy combine
  To form a life, whose holy springs
    Are hidden and divine.

3 Their pleasures rise from things unseen,
    Beyond this world and time,
  Where neither eyes nor ears have been,
    Nor thoughts of mortals climb.

4 They want no pomp nor royal throne
    To raise their honours here;
  Content and pleas'd to live unknown
    Till Christ their life appear.

HYMN CXI.
The Christian's Prospect.

1 HAPPY the soul, whose wishes climb
  To mansions in the skies!
He looks on all the joys of time
  With undesiring eyes.

2 In vain soft Pleasure spreads her charms,
  And throws her silken chain;
And Wealth and Fame invite his arms,
  And tempt his ear, in vain.

3 He knows that all these glittering things
  Must yield to sure decay;
And sees, on Time's extended wings,
  How swift they fleet away.

4 To things, unseen by mortal eyes,
  A beam of sacred light
Directs his views; his prospects rise
  All permanent and bright.

5 His hopes, still fix'd on joys to come,
  Those blissful scenes on high,
Shall flourish in immortal bloom,
  When time and nature die.

HYMN CXII.
The acceptable Sacrifice.

1 WHEREWITH shall I approach the Lord,
  And bow before his throne?
Or how procure his kind regard,
  And for my guilt atone?

e Shall

2 Shall altars flame, and victims bleed,
    And spicy fumes ascend?
Will these my earnest wish succeed,
    And make my God my friend?

3 Oh! no, my soul, 'twere fruitless all,
    Such off'rings are in vain;
No fatlings, from the field or stall,
    His favour can obtain.

4 To men their rights I must allow,
    And proofs of kindness give;
To God with humble rev'rence bow,
    And to his glory live.

5 Hands that are clean, and hearts sincere,
    He never will despise;
And cheerful duty he'll prefer
    To costly sacrifice.

HYMN CXIII.

The Citizen of Sion.

1 WHO shall to thy chosen seat
    Turn in glad approach his feet?
Who, great God, a welcome guest
On thy hallow'd mountain rest?

2 He whose heart thy love has warm'd;
He whose will to thine conform'd,
Bids his life unsullied run;
He whose word and thought are one;

3 He who ne'er, with cruel aim,
Seeks to wound an honest fame;
Nor to slander's tongue severe
Lends with easy faith his ear;

4 Who, from servile terror free,
　Turns from those who turn from thee;
　And to each, who thee obeys,
　Love and honour ever pays;

5 What he swears, with stedfast will
　Ever ready to fulfil;
　Nor can bribes his sentence guide
　'Gainst the guiltless to decide;

6 He who thus, with heart unstain'd,
　Treads the path by thee ordain'd,
　He, great God, shall own thy care,
　And thy constant blessing share.

HYMN CXIV.
The Advantage of early Religion.

1 HAPPY the soul, whose early years
　　Receives instruction well;
　Who hates the sinner's path, and fears
　　The road that leads to hell.

2 When we devote our youth to God,
　　'Tis pleasing in his eyes;
　A flower, when offer'd in the bud,
　　Is no vain sacrifice.

3 'Tis easier work, if we begin
　　To fear the Lord betimes;
　While sinners, who grow old in sin,
　　Are harden'd in their crimes.

4 'Twill save us from a thousand snares,
　　To mind religion young;
　Grace will preserve our following years,
　　And make our virtue strong.

HYMN CXV.

Remember thy Creator in the days of thy Youth.

1 IN the soft season of thy youth,
　　In nature's smiling bloom,
　Ere age arrive, and trembling wait
　　Its summons to the tomb;

2 Remember thy Creator God;
　　For him thy powers employ;
　Make him thy fear, thy love, thy hope,
　　Thy confidence, thy joy.

3 He shall defend and guide thy course
　　Thro' life's uncertain sea,
　Till thou art landed on the shore
　　Of blest eternity.

4 Then seek the Lord betimes, and choose
　　The path of heav'nly truth;
　The earth affords no lovelier sight
　　Than a religious youth.

HYMN CXVI.

Gravity and Decency.

1 CAN laughter feed th' immortal mind?
　　Were spirits of celestial kind
　Made for a jest, for sport, and play,
　　To wear out time, and waste the day?

2 Doth vain discourse, or empty mirth,
　　Well suit the honours of their birth?
　Shall they be fond of gay attire,
　　Which children love, and fools admire?

3 What if we wear the richest vest?
  Peacocks and flies are better drest;
  This flesh, with all its gaudy forms,
  Must drop to dust, and feed the worms.

4 Lord, raise our hearts and passions higher;
  Touch all our souls with sacred fire;
  Then, with a heaven-directed eye,
  We'll pass these glittering trifles by.

5 We'll look on all the toys below
  With such disdain as angels do;
  And wait the call that bids us rise
  To mansions promis'd in the skies.

HYMN CXVII.
Contentment. *Beautiful*

1 IF solid happiness we prize,
    Within our breasts this jewel lies,
      Unwise are they who roam;
  The world has nothing to bestow,
  From our own selves our joys must flow,
      And peace begins at home.

2 We'll therefore relish with content
  Whate'er kind Providence hath sent,
      Nor aim beyond our pow'r;
  And, if our store of wealth be small,
  With thankful hearts enjoy it all,
      Nor lose the present hour.

3 To be resign'd, when ills betide,
  Patient, when favours are deny'd,
      And pleas'd with favours giv'n;
  This is the wise, the virtuous part,
  This is that incense of the heart,
      Whose fragrance reaches heav'n.

4 Thus, crown'd with peace, thro' life we'll go,
    Its chequer'd paths of joy and wo
        With cautious steps we'll tread;
    Quit its vain scenes without a tear,
    Without a trouble or a fear,
        And mingle with the dead.

5 While Conscience, like a faithful friend,
    Shall thro' the gloomy vale attend,
        And cheer our dying breath;
    Shall, when all other comforts cease,
    Like a kind angel whisper peace,
        And smooth the bed of death.

HYMN CXVIII.
Patience.

1 PATIENCE, O 'tis a grace divine
    Sent from the God of pow'r and love,
  That leans upon its father's arm,
  As thro' the wilds of life we rove.

2 By patience we serenely bear
  The troubles of our mortal state,
  And wait contented our discharge,
  Nor think our glory comes too late.

3 O for this grace to aid us on,
  And arm with fortitude the breast,
  Till, life's tumultuous voyage o'er,
  We reach the shores of endless rest.

4 Faith into vision shall resign,
  Hope shall in full fruition die,
  And patience in possession end,
  In the bright worlds of bliss on high.

HYMN CXIX.
Prudence.

'Tis a lovely thing to see
   A man of prudent heart,
Whose thoughts, and lips, and life, agree
   To act a useful part.

When envy, strife and wars begin,
   In little angry souls,
Mark how the sons of peace come in,
   And quench the kindling coals.

Their minds are humble, mild and meek,
   Nor let their anger rise;
Nor passion moves their lips to speak,
   Nor pride exalts their eyes.

Their lives are prudence mix'd with love;
   Good works employ their day;
They join the serpent with the dove,
   But cast the sting away.

HYMN CXX.
Equity.

My soul, abjure th' accursed throng,
   Whose prosp'ring wealth increases fast
By fraud, by violence, and wrong,
Still thriving for the thunder's blast.

If high or low my station be,
Of noble or ignoble name,
By uncorrupted honesty
Thy blessing, Lord, I'd humbly claim.

3 Enrich'd with that, no want I'll fear,
Thy providence shall be my trust;
Thou wilt provide my portion here,
Thou friend and guardian of the just.

4 O may I, with sincere delight,
To all the task of duty pay;
Tender of every social right,
Obedient to thy righteous sway.

5 Such virtue thou wilt not forget,
In worlds where every virtue shares
A fit reward, tho' not of debt,
But what thy boundless grace prepares.

HYMN CXXI.
Liberality.

1 HAPPY is he who fears the Lord,
And follows his commands;
Who lends the poor without reward,
Or gives with lib'ral hands.

2 As pity dwells within his breast
To all the sons of need,
So God shall answer his request
With blessings on his seed.

3 No evil tidings shall surprise
His well establish'd mind;
His soul to God his refuge flies,
And leaves his fears behind.

4 In times of general distress,
Some beams of light shall shine,
To shew the world his righteousness,
And give him peace divine.

His works of piety and love
　Remain before the Lord;
Honour on earth, and joy above,
　Shall be his sure reward.

HYMN CXXII.

Christian Unity.

LET party strife no more
　The Christian world o'erspread;
Gentile and Jew, and Bond and Free,
　Are one in Christ their head.

Among the saints on earth
　Let mutual love be found;
Heirs of the same inheritance,
　With mutual blessings crown'd.

Let discord, child of hell,
　Be banish'd far away;
Those should in strictest friendship dwell,
　Who the same Lord obey.

Thus will the Church below
　Resemble that above,
Where streams of pleasure ever flow,
　And ev'ry heart is love.

HYMN CXXIII.
Brotherly Love.

1 O GOD, our Father, and our King;
Of all we have, or hope, the spring;
Send down thy spirit from above,
And warm our hearts with holy love.

2 May we from every act abstain,
That hurts or gives our neighbour pain;
And ev'ry secret wish suppress,
That would abridge his happiness.

3 Still may we feel our hearts inclin'd
To act the friend to all our kind;
Still seek their safety, health and ease,
Virtue, eternal life, and peace.

4 With pity let our breast o'erflow,
When we behold a wretch in wo;
And bear a sympathizing part
With all who are of heavy heart.

5 Let love in all our conduct shine,
An image fair, tho' faint of thine:
Thus may we Christ's disciples prove,
Who came to manifest thy love.

HYMN CXXIV.
Love to Mankind recommended by Christ.

1 BEHOLD where, breathing love divine,
Our dying Master stands!
His weeping followers, gathering round,
Receive his last commands.

2 From

2 From that mild Teacher's parting lips
    What tender accents fell!
The gentle precept which he gave
    Became its Author well.

3 Bleſt is the man, whoſe ſoft'ning heart
    Feels all another's pain;
To whom the ſupplicating eye
    Was never rais'd in vain:

4 Whoſe breaſt expands with generous warmth,
    A ſtranger's woes to feel;
And bleeds in pity o'er the wound
    He wants the power to heal.

5 To gentle offices of love
    His feet are never ſlow;
He views, thro' mercy's melting eye,
    A brother in a foe.

6 To him protection ſhall be ſhewn,
    And mercy from above
Deſcend on thoſe who thus fulfil
    The perfect law of love.

HYMN CXXV.
Religion vain, without Love.

1 HAD we the tongues of Greeks or Jews,
    And nobler ſpeech than Angels uſe,
If love be wanting, we are found,
Like tinkling braſs, an empty ſound.

2 Were we inſpir'd to preach and tell
All that is done in heaven and hell,
Or could our faith the world remove,
Still we are nothing, without love.

3 Should

3 Should we distribute all our store
  To cheer the bowels of the poor,
  Or give our bodies to the flame
  To gain a martyr's glorious name:

4 If love to God and love to man
  Be absent, all our hopes are vain;
  Nor tongues, nor gifts, nor fiery zeal,
  The work of love can e'er fulfil.

HYMN CXXVI.
Domestick Love.

1 LO, what an entertaining sight
    Are kindred who agree!
How blest the house, where hearts unite
    In bands of piety!

2 Where streams of love, from heav'nly springs,
    Descend on every soul;
And sacred peace, with balmy wings,
    Shades and bedews the whole!

3 All in their proper stations move,
    And each fulfils his part,
In all the cares of life and love,
    With sympathizing heart.

4 Their souls are form'd for joy and peace,
    Their hearts and hopes are one;
And kind desires, to serve and please,
    Thro' all their actions run.

5 How happy is the pious house,
    Where zeal and friendship meet;
Where songs of praise, and mingled vows,
    Make the communion sweet!

6 Such pleasure crowns the heav'nly hills;
　　Thus saints are blest above;
　Where joy like morning dew distils,
　　And all the air is love.

HYMN CXXVII.
The Beatitudes.

1 BLESS'D are the humble souls, who see
　　Their emptiness and poverty;
　Treasures of grace to them are given,
　And crowns of joy laid up in heaven.

2 Bless'd are the men of broken heart,
　Who mourn for sin with inward smart;
　From heaven the streams of mercy flow,
　An healing balm for all their wo.

3 Bless'd are the men who thirst for grace,
　Hunger and long for righteousness;
　They shall be well supply'd and fed
　With living streams, and living bread.

4 Bless'd are the men of peaceful life,
　Who quench the coals of growing strife;
　They shall be call'd the heirs of bliss,
　The sons of God, the God of peace.

5 Bless'd are the men whose bowels move,
　And melt with sympathy and love;
　From God, their Lord, shall they obtain
　Like sympathy and love again.

6 Bless'd are the pure, whose hearts are clean
   From the defiling powers of sin;
   With endless pleasure shall they see
   A God of spotless purity.

7 Bless'd are the men who now partake
   Of shame and pain, for Jesus' sake;
   Their souls, exulting in the Lord,
   Shall share at last a just reward.

HYMN CXXVIII.

The different Character of the Righteous and Wicked.

1 HOW greatly bless'd the man, whose ear
      The sinner's council shuns to hear;
   And where the sons of folly stray,
   Declines his studious steps the way.

2 Nor frantic mirth he deigns to share,
   Nor sits he in the scorner's chair;
   His heart, possess'd with sacred awe,
   Daily revolves God's holy law.

3 Like a fair tree, that, taught to grow
   Where living streams of water flow,
   His fruitful branch he rears on high,
   Nor fears a sickening autumn nigh.

4 Whate'er his ready thoughts devise,
   He, joyful, to the work applies;
   Still sure to find the wish'd success
   Repay his hope, his labour bless.

HYMN CXXIX.
The Blessedness of true Penitence.

1 BEYOND expression blest is he
    Whose num'rous sins are cover'd o'er;
The humble soul, to whom the Lord
    Imputes his guilty deeds no more.

2 He mourns his sinful follies past,
    And keeps his heart with constant care;
His lips and life, without deceit,
    Shall prove his penitence sincere.

3 The man, who hides his conscious guilt,
    Shall pine beneath a secret wound;
But he, who owns and leaves his faults,
    With peace and pardon shall be crown'd.

4 The Lord hath built a throne of grace,
    Free to dispense his mercies there,
That sinners may approach his face,
    And hope and love, as well as fear.

HYMN CXXX.
The Gospel Invitation to penitent Sinners.

1 COME, weary souls, with sin distrest;
    To you is offer'd heavenly rest;
The kind, the gracious call obey,
    And cast your gloomy fears away.

2 Oppress'd with guilt, a painful load,
    O come, and spread your woes abroad;
Divine compassion, mighty love,
    Will all the painful load remove.

3 Here mercy's boundless ocean flows,
To cleanse your guilt and heal your woes;
Pardon, and life, and endless peace—
How rich the gift! how free the grace!

4 Come and accept, with thankful hearts,
The hope which heavenly grace imparts;
O come with trembling, yet rejoice,
And bless the kind inviting voice.

5 Great God! O may thy powerful love
Confirm our faith, our fears remove,
And sweetly influence every breast,
And guide us to eternal rest!

HYMN CXXXI.
Now is the Day of Salvation.

1 THE swift declining day,
  How fast its moments fly!
While evening's broad and gloomy shade
  Gains on the western sky.

2 Ye mortals, mark its pace,
  And use the hours of light;
And know its Maker can command
  An instantaneous night.

3 His word blots out the sun
  In its meridian blaze,
And cuts from smiling vigorous youth
  The remnant of its days.

4 On the dark mountain's brow
  Your feet may quickly slide,
And from its dreadful summit dash
  Your momentary pride.

HYMN CXXXII.
The God of Mercy.

1 BLEST be the grace which did proclaim,
   O Lord of hosts, thy holy name;
   " The Lord, the gracious Lord,
   " Long-suffering, merciful and kind;
   " The God who always bears in mind
   " His everlasting word.

2 " Plenteous he is in truth and grace;
   " He wills that all our sinful race
   " Should turn, repent, and live;
   " His pardoning grace for all is free,
   " Transgression, sin, iniquity,
   " He freely doth forgive."

3 O then that every sinful soul,
   By faith and penitence made whole,
   May know their sins forgiven;
   The proffer'd benefits embrace,
   The plenitude of gospel grace,
   The antepast of heaven!

4 Be this our one great business here,
   With serious industry and care
   Our future bliss to ensure;
   Thine utmost counsel to fulfil,
   And suffer all thy righteous will,
   And to the end endure.

HYMN CXXXIII.
The Shortness of human Life.

1 FRAIL is the state of mortal man,
   His life's a shade, his days a span,
  He can't prolong his vital breath,
  Nor 'scape the unerring shaft of death.

2 Soon he declines from youth to age,
And passes swiftly o'er the stage;
Swift from the cradle to the tomb,
From sprightly spring to winter's gloom.

3 Be ever watchful, then, my soul,
While days, and months, and seasons roll;
Redeem the present fleeting hour,
Improve it while 'tis in thy power:

4 That when this transient life's no more,
And all its joys and cares are o'er,
From death's dark vale thou may'st arise
To nobler mansions in the skies.

HYMN CXXXIV.
The Frailty of human Life.

1 LO what a feeble frame is ours!
   How vain a thing is man!
How frail are all our boasted pow'rs!
   And short at best our span!

2 Swift as the feather'd arrow flies,
   And cuts the yielding air;
Or as a kindling meteor dies,
   Ere it can well appear:

3 So pass our fleeting years away,
   And time runs on its race;
In vain we ask a moment's stay,
   Nor will it slack its pace.

4 O make us truly wise to learn
   How very frail we are;
That we may mind our grand concern,
   And for our death prepare.

HYMN CXXXV. *Beautiful*

The Frailty and Shortness of Life.

1 LORD, what a feeble piece
   Is this our mortal frame!
Our life, how poor a trifle 'tis,
   That scarce deserves the name!

2 Alas, the brittle clay,
   That built our body first!
And ev'ry month, and every day,
   'Tis mould'ring back to dust.

3 Our moments fly apace,
   Nor will our minutes stay;
Just like a flood our hasty days
   Are sweeping us away.

4 Well, if our days must fly,
   We'll keep their end in sight;
We'll spend them all in wisdom's way,
   And let them speed their flight.

5 They'll waft us sooner o'er
   This life's tempestuous sea;
Soon we shall reach the peaceful shore
   Of blest eternity.

HYMN CXXXVI.

So teach us to number our Days, that we may apply our Hearts unto Wisdom.

1 TO-morrow, Lord, is thine,
   Lodg'd in thy sovereign hand;
And if its sun arise and shine,
   It shines by thy command.

2 The present moment flies,
  And bears our life away;
O make thy servants truly wise,
  'That they may live to day.

3 One thing demands our care;
  O be it still pursu'd!
Lest, slighted once, the season fair
  Should never be renew'd.

4 To thee O may we fly,
  Swift as the morning light!
Lest life's young golden beams should die
  In sudden, endless night.

HYMN CXXXVII.
Redeeming the Time.

1 GOD of eternity, from thee
  Did infant time its being draw;
Moments, and days, and months, and years,
Revolve by thine unvaried law.

2 Silent and slow they glide away;
Steady and strong the current flows;
Lost in eternity's vast sea,
The boundless gulf from whence it rose.

3 With it the thoughtless sons of men
Before the rapid streams are borne,
On to that everlasting home,
Whence not one soul can e'er return.

4 Yet while the shore on either side
Presents a gaudy, flatt'ring shew,
They gaze, in fond amusement lost,
Nor think to what a world they go.

5 Great

5 Great Source of Wisdom, teach our heart
To know the price of every hour;
That time may bear us on to joys
Beyond its measure and its power.

HYMN CXXXVIII.

It is appointed unto all Men once to die.

1 BEHOLD the path which mortals tread
Down to the regions of the dead!
Nor will the fleeting moments stay,
Nor can we measure back our way.

2 From vital air, from cheerful light,
To the cold grave's perpetual night;
From scenes of duty, means of grace,
I must to God's tribunal pass.

3 Awake, my soul! thy way prepare,
And lose in this each mortal care;
With steady feet that path be trod,
Which thro' the grave conducts to God.

4 Then shall I smile secure from fear,
Tho' death should blast the rising year;
And joy to meet the blissful shore,
From whence I shall return no more.

HYMN CXXXIX.
Death the Lot of all Mankind.

1 DEath calls our friends, our neighbours, hence,
And none refist the fatal dart;
Continual warnings ftrike our fenfe—
And fhall they fail to reach our heart?

2 That awful hour will foon appear,
(Swift on the wings of time it flies)
When all that pains or pleafes, here,
Shall vanifh from our clofing eyes.

3 Lord of our life, infpire our heart
With heav'nly ardour, grace divine;
Nor let thy prefence e'er depart,
For ftrength, and life, and death, are thine.

4 O teach us the celeftial fkill
Each awful warning to improve;
And, while our days are fhort'ning ftill,
Prepare us for the joys above.

HYMN CXL.
Mortality.

1 SOV'REIGN of life! before thine eye,
Lo, mortal men by thoufands die!
One glance from thee at once brings down
The proudeft brow that wears a crown!

2 Banifh'd at once from human fight,
To the dark grave's unchanging night,
Imprifon'd in that dufty bed,
We hide our folitary head.

3 The friendly band no more shall greet,
  (Accents familiar once, and sweet!)
  No more the well-known features trace,
  No more renew the fond embrace.

4 Yet, if our Father's faithful hand
  Conduct us thro' this gloomy land,
  Our souls with pleasure shall obey,
  And follow where he leads the way.

5 He, nobler friends than here we leave,
  In brighter, surer worlds, can give;
  Or, by the beamings of his eye,
  A lost creation well supply.

HYMN CXLI.
God our Guardian in Life and Death.

1   THY everlasting truth,
      Father, thy ceaseless love,
  Sees all thy children's wants, and knows
      What best for each will prove.

2   And whatsoe'er thou will'st
      Thou do'st, O King of Kings!
  What thine unerring wisdom chose,
      Thy power to being brings.

3   Thou every where hast way,
      And all things serve thy might;
  Thy every act pure blessing is,
      Thy path unsullied light.

4   When thou arisest, Lord,
      What shall thy work withstand?
  When all thy children want thou giv'st,
      Who, who shall stay thy hand?

5 Thou seest our weakness, Lord;
    Our hearts are known to thee;
  O lift thou up the sinking hand,
    Confirm the feeble knee.

6 Let us, in life, and death,
    Thy stedfast truth declare,
  And publish, with our latest breath,
    Thy love and guardian care.

HYMN CXLII.
Comfort in Sickness and Death.

1 WHEN sickness shakes the languid frame,
      Each dazzling pleasure flies;
  Phantoms of bliss no more obscure
      Our long deluded eyes.

2 Then the tremendous arm of death
      Its fatal sceptre shews;
  And nature faints beneath the weight
      Of complicated woes.

3 The tott'ring frame of mortal life
      Shall crumble into dust;
  Nature shall faint—but learn, my soul,
      On nature's God to trust.

4 The man, whose pious heart is fix'd
      On his all-gracious God,
  From ev'ry frown may draw a joy,
      And kiss the chast'ning rod.

5 Nor him shall death itself alarm;
      On heav'n his soul relies;
  With joy he views his Maker's love,
      And with composure dies.

HYMN

HYMN CXLIII.
The Hope of future Blessedness.

1 COME, ye who love the Lord,
   And let your joys be known;
 Join in a song with sweet accord,
   While ye surround his throne.

2 Let those refuse to sing,
   Who never knew our God;
 But servants of the heavenly King
   May speak their joys abroad.

3 The men of grace have found
   Glory begun below;
 Celestial fruits on earthly ground
   From faith and hope may grow.

4 Then let our songs abound,
   And every tear be dry;
 We're marching thro' this present world
   To fairer worlds on high.

HYMN CXLIV.
A View of Futurity. Beautifull

1 NOW let our souls, on wings sublime,
   Rise from the vanities of time;
 Draw back the parting veil, and see
 The glories of eternity.

2 Born by a new, celestial birth,
 Why should we grovel here on earth?
 Why grasp at transitory toys,
 So near to heaven's eternal joys?

3 Shall ought beguile us on the road,
　When we are walking back to God ?
　For strangers into life we come,
　And dying is but going home.

4 To dwell with God, to feel his love,
　Is the full heaven enjoy'd above ;
　And the sweet expectation now
　Is the young dawn of heaven below.

HYMN CXLV. *Beautiful*

The Prospect of Heaven a Support in Death.

1 THERE is a land of pure delight,
　　Where saints immortal reign ;
　Infinite day excludes the night,
　　And pleasures banish pain.

2 There everlasting spring abides,
　　And never-fading flowers ;
　Death, like a narrow sea, divides
　　This heavenly land from ours.

3 Sweet fields, beyond the swelling flood,
　　Stand dress'd in living green ;
　So to the Jews old Canaan stood,
　　While Jordan roll'd between.

4 But fearful mortals start, and shrink,
　　To cross this narrow sea ;
　And linger, shiv'ring, on the brink,
　　And fear to launch away.

5 Oh ! could we make our doubts remove,
　　Those gloomy doubts that rise,
　And see the Canaan that we love,
　　With unbeclouded eyes ;

6 Could

6 Could we but climb where Moses stood,
   And view the landscape o'er—
Not Jordan's streams, or death's cold flood,
   Should fright us from the shore.

HYMN CXLVI.
Behold the Lamb of God!

1 BEHOLD the Lamb of God!
   The holy Baptist cries;
Whilst joy inspir'd his pious breast,
   And sparkled in his eyes.

2 Let us behold the Lamb;
   In him no spot we see;
How patient, gentle, meek and mild!
   From guile, from error free.

3 See Jesus, like a lamb
   Led to the sacrifice;
And silent as the sheep which dumb
   Before his shearer lies.

4 Behold this spotless Lamb!
   And mark the path he trod!
That blessed road will surely lead
   To happiness and God.

HYMN CXLVII.
The Promise is unto you and your Children.

1 LORD, what our ears have heard,
   Our eyes, delighted, trace;
Thy love, in long succession, shewn
   To Sion's chosen race:
   Our children dost thou claim,
   And mark them out for thine!
Ten thousand blessings to thy name,
   For goodness so divine!

2   Thee let the fathers own,
      And thee the sons adore;
   Join'd to the Lord in solemn vows,
      To be forgot no more:
   Thy cov'nant may they keep,
      And bless the happy bands,
   Which closer still engage their hearts
      To honour thy commands.

3   How great thy mercies, Lord!
      How plenteous is thy grace!
   Which, in the promise of thy love,
      Includes each rising race:
   Our offspring, still thy care,
      Shall own their fathers' God;
   To latest time thy blessing share,
      And sound thy praise abroad.

4   But weak our noblest praise,
      For favours such as thine;
   O how can tongues of feeble clay
      Proclaim the love divine!
   We wonder and adore!
      And, to exalt such grace,
   We long to learn the songs of heaven,
      Before we reach the place.

HYMN CXLVIII.

God the Dwelling-Place of his People through all Generations.

1   THOU, Lord, thro' ev'ry changing scene,
      Hast to thy flock a refuge been;
   Thro' ev'ry age, eternal God,
      Their pleasing home, their safe abode.

2 In thee our fathers fought their reft,
  In thee our fathers now are bleft:
  Lo, we are rifen (a tranfient race)
  A while to fill our fathers' place.

3 While travelling thro' life's varied road,
  We lean upon our fathers' God;
  On thee our ftedfaft hopes recline,
  Nor own, nor afk, a help but thine.

4 To thee our infant race we give;
  Them may their fathers' God receive;
  By fweet experience let them prove
  Thy mercy, thine unchanging love.

5 Thus voices yet unform'd fhall raife
  A grateful tribute to thy praife;
  Our children learn the joyful fong,
  And theirs the cheerful notes prolong.

6 Thou Saviour of the human race!
  Thou Fountain of exhauftlefs Grace!
  Thy mercy ages paft have known,
  And ages long to come fhall own.

7 So fhall thy love, in ftrains fublime,
  Be fung to the laft hour of time:
  Then fhall eternity confefs,
  Thro' all its rounds, thy matchlefs grace.

HYMN CXLIX.

Family Devotion.

1 FATHER of all! thy care we blefs,
    Which crowns our families with peace:
  From thee they fpring, and by thy hand
  They have been, and are ftill, fuftain'd.

2 To God, moſt worthy to be prais'd,
  Be our domeſtick altars rais'd,
  Who, Lord of heav'n, ſcorns not to dwell
  With ſaints in their obſcureſt cell.

3 To thee may each united houſe
  With joy preſent its grateful vows;
  Our ſervants, there, and riſing race,
  Be taught thy precepts and thy grace.

4 O may each future age proclaim
  The honours of thy glorious name!
  While, pleas'd and thankful, we remove
  To join thy family above.

HYMN CL.
The Bleſſing of a Goſpel Miniſtry.

1 HOW bleſt are they, how truly wiſe,
  Who learn and keep the ſacred road!
  Happy the men whom Heav'n employs
  To turn rebellious hearts to God!

2 While theſe declare the written word,
  And prove their doctrine from the Lord,
  To him, in them, reſpect we'll pay,
  And bleſs the doctrines they convey.

3 Let them inſtruct—we would be wiſe;
  Their juſt reproofs we'll not deſpiſe;
  But meet with love their faithful cares,
  And join with them our fervent prayers.

4 May peace from heav'n upon them reſt,
  And be their labours greatly bleſt,
  To ſave from ſin, ſad hearts relieve—
  And may they ſhare the joys they give.

HYMN

HYMN CLI.
Christian Fellowship.

1 ABBA, Father, God of love!
   Send thy blessing from above;
Light and life to all impart;
Shine on each believing heart;
Kindly comfort all who mourn,
Into joy their sorrow turn;

2 Joy which none can take away,
Joy which shall for ever stay;
All thy kingdom from above,
All the happiness of love;
Be it to thy servants given,
Pardon, holiness, and heaven.

3 Glorious in thy saints appear,
Plant thy heavenly kingdom here;
Faith and love and joy increase,
Temperance and gentleness;
Plant in us an humble mind,
Patient, pitiful, and kind;

4 Meek and lowly let us be,
Full of goodness, full of thee;
Make us all in thee complete,
Make us all for glory meet,
Meet to appear before thy sight,
Partners with the saints in light.

5 Let us, in our spirits, prove
All the depths of humble love;
Let us, in our lives, express
All the heights of holiness;
To thy church the pattern give,
Shew how true believers live.

6 When the glorious race is run,
  Fought the fight, the battle won;
  Let us then with joy remove
  To thy family above;
  On the wings of angels fly,
  Shew how true believers die.

HYMN CLII.

A Funeral Hymn.

1 THE God of love will sure indulge
  The flowing tear, the heaving sigh,
  When righteous persons fall around,
  When tender friends and kindred die.

2 Yet not one anxious murmuring thought
  Should with our mourning passions blend;
  Nor should our bleeding hearts forget
  Th' Almighty ever-living friend.

3 Beneath a numerous train of ills,
  Our feeble flesh and heart may fail;
  Yet shall our hope in thee, our God,
  O'er every gloomy fear prevail.

4 Parent and husband, guard and guide,
  Thou art each tender name in one;
  On thee we cast our every care,
  And comfort seek from thee alone.

5 Our Father, God, to thee we look;
  Our rock, our portion, and our friend;
  And on thy gracious love and truth,
  Our sinking souls shall still depend.

HYMN CLIII.
The Mission of Christ.

1 HARK the glad sound, the Saviour comes!
  The Saviour, promis'd long;
Let ev'ry heart a throne prepare,
  And ev'ry voice a song!

2 On him the Spirit, largely shed,
  Exerts its sacred fire;
Wisdom and might, and zeal and love,
  His holy breast inspire.

3 He comes, the pris'ners to relieve,
  In Satan's bondage held;
The gates of brass before him burst,
  The iron fetters yield.

4 He comes, from thickest clouds of vice
  To clear the darken'd mind;
And, from on high, a saving light
  To pour upon the blind.

5 He comes, the broken hearts to bind,
  The bleeding souls to cure;
And, with the treasures of his grace,
  T' enrich the humble poor.

HYMN CLIV.
The Divine Power and Energy.

1 AUTHOR of every work divine,
  Who dost thro' both creations shine,
The God of nature and of grace,
Thy glorious steps in all we see,
And wisdom attribute to thee,
  And power, and majesty, and praise.

2 That

2 That all-informing breath thou art,
Who doſt continued life impart,
   And bidſt the world perſiſt to be;
Garniſh'd by thee yon azure ſky;
And all thoſe beauteous orbs on high
   Depend in golden chains from thee.

3 Thou doſt create the earth anew,
Its Maker and Preſerver too,
   By thine almighty arm ſuſtain;
Nature perceives thy ſecret force,
And ſtill holds on her even courſe,
   And owns thy providential reign.

4 Thou art the Univerſal Soul,
The plaſtick power that fills the whole,
   And governs earth, air, ſea, and ſky;
The creatures all thy breath receive,
And who by thy inſpiring live,
   Without thy inſpiration die.

5 Spirit immenſe, eternal Mind!
Thou on the ſouls of all mankind
   Doſt with benigneſt influence move;
Pleas'd to reſtore a ſinful race,
And new create a world of grace
   In all the image of thy love.

HYMN CLV.
The Divine Influence implored.

1 FATHER of everlaſting love,
   Take to thyſelf thy mighty power;
Let all earth's ſons thy mercies prove,
   Let all thy wond'rous grace adore.

2 The triumphs of thy love diſplay,
   In every heart reign thou alone,
Till all thy foes confeſs thy ſway,
   And glory ends what grace begun.

3 The God of grace, and health, and power,
   Fountain of light and love below,
Abroad thine healing influence ſhower,
   O'er all the nations let it flow.

4 Inflame our hearts with perfect love,
   In us the work of faith fulfil;
So not heaven's hoſt ſhall ſwifter move,
   Than we on earth, to do thy will.

HYMN CLVI.
God is Light.

1 FOUNTAIN of uncreated light!
     Thou giver of the mental ſight!
   Thy beams on all are ſhed;
Thy grace, on all mankind beſtow'd,
Still points each ſeeking ſoul the road
   To happineſs and God.

2 Lighten'd by thine interior ray,
  Thee ev'ry child of Adam may
     His unknown God explore,
   And, following cloſe thy ſecret grace,
   Immerge into that glorious place
      Where darkneſs is no more.

3 The univerſal light thou art,
   And turn'd to thee the darkeſt heart
      A glimmering ſpark may find;
   Let man reject it or embrace,
   Thou offereſt thy ſaving grace
      To us and all mankind.

4 Light of our soul, we follow thee
In humble faith on earth to see
   Thy perfect day of love,
And then with all thy saints in light
To gain the beatifick sight
   Which makes their heaven above.

HYMN CLVII.
For New Year's Day.

1 GOD of our life! thy constant care
   With blessings crowns each rising year:
This feeble life thou dost prolong,
And wake anew our annual song.

2 How many precious souls are fled
To the vast regions of the dead,
Since from this day the changing sun
Thro' his last yearly period run!

3 We yet survive—but who can say,
Or thro' the year, or month, or day,
He shall retain his vital breath?
Thus far, at least, in league with death!

4 That breath is thine, eternal God!
'Tis thine to fix the soul's abode:
We hold our life from thee alone,
On earth, or in the world unknown.

5 To thee our spirits we resign:
O make and own them still as thine!
So shall they smile, secure from fear,
Tho' death should blast the rising year.

6 Thy children, eager to be gone,
Bid time's impetuous tide roll on,
And land them on that happy shore
Where sin and death are known no more.

HYMN CLVIII.

For the Beginning of a New Year.

1 GREAT God! we sing that mighty hand,
  By which supported still we stand:
  The opening year thy mercy shows,
  Thy mercy crowns it till it close.

2 By day, by night, at home, abroad,
  Still are we guarded by our God,
  By thine incessant bounty fed,
  By thine unerring counsel led.

3 With grateful hearts the past we own;
  The future, all to us unknown,
  We to thy guardian care submit,
  And peaceful leave before thy feet.

4 In scenes exalted, or depress'd,
  Thou art our joy, and thou our rest;
  Thy goodness all our hopes shall raise,
  Ador'd thro' all our changing days.

5 When death shall interrupt these songs,
  And seal in silence mortal tongues,
  Our helper God, in whom we trust,
  In better worlds, our souls shall boast.

HYMN CLIX.

Thanksgiving for National Peace.

1 NOW let our songs address the God of peace,
  Who bids the tumult of the battle cease!
  The pointed spears to pruning crooks he bends,
  And the broad faulchion in the ploughshare ends:
His powerful bands unite contending nations
In kind embrace, and friendly salutations.

2 While we beneath our vines and fig-trees sit,
    Or thus within thy sacred temple meet,
    Accept, great God! the tribute of our song,
    And all the mercies of this day prolong:
Then spread thy peaceful word thro' ev'ry nation,
That all the earth may hail thy great salvation.

HYMN CLX.
Thanksgiving for Peace.

1 GREAT Ruler of the earth and skies!
    A word of thy almighty breath
  Can sink the world, or bid it rise;
    Thy smile is life, thy frown is death.

2 When angry nations rush to arms,
    And rage, and noise, and tumult, reign,
  And war resounds its dire alarms,
    And slaughter spreads the hostile plain;

3 Thy sov'reign eye looks calmly down,
    And marks their course, and bounds their pow'r;
  Thy word the angry nations own,
    And noise and war are heard no more.

4 Then peace returns with balmy wing,
    (Sweet peace! with her what blessings fled!)
  Glad plenty laughs, the vallies sing,
    Reviving commerce lifts her head.

5 Thou good, and wise, and righteous Lord!
    All move subservient to thy will;
  And peace and war await thy word,
    And thy sublime decree fulfil.

6 To thee we pay our grateful songs,
    Thy kind protection still implore:
  O may our hearts, and lives, and tongues,
    Confess thy goodness, and adore!

HYMN CLXI.
Thanks for National Protection.

O Come, let us sing to the Lord a new song,
And praise him to whom all our praises belong!
While we enter his temple with gladness and joy,
Let a psalm of thanksgiving our voices employ!
O come, to his name let us joyfully sing!
For the Lord is a great and omnipotent King;
By his word were the heavens & the host of them made,
And of the round world the foundation he laid.

He stilleth the waves of the boisterous sea,
And the tumults of men, more outrageous than they:
Thy goodness, O Lord! let the people confess,
Whom wars do not waste, nor proud tyrants oppress,
And devoutly contemplate thy wonderful ways,
Thou who turnest the fierceness of men to thy praise!
Then our lands in due season shall yield their increase,
And the Lord give his people the blessings of peace.

HYMN CLXII.
The Blessing of Civil Government.

1 ETERNAL, sov'reign Lord on high,
    And Lord of all below!
We mortals to thy Majesty
    Our first obedience owe.

2 Our souls adore thy pow'r supreme,
    And bless thy providence,
For magistrates of meaner name,
    Our glory and defence.

3 Kingdoms on firm foundations stand,
    While virtue finds reward;
And sinners perish from the land,
    By justice and the sword.

4 Where

4 Where laws and liberties combine
    To make a people bleſt,
There crowns with brighteſt luſtre ſhine,
    And kings are honour'd beſt.

5 Let Cæſar's due be ever paid
    To Cæſar and his throne;
But conſciences and ſouls were made
    For thee, O God! alone.

HYMN CLXIII.
Univerſal Prayer. *Beautiful*

1 FATHER of all! in ev'ry age,
    In ev'ry clime ador'd,
By ſaint, by ſavage, and by ſage,
    JEHOVAH, JOVE, or LORD!

2 Thou great Firſt Cauſe! leaſt underſtood!
    Who all my ſenſe confin'd
To know but this—that thou art good,
    And that myſelf am blind;

3 Yet gave me, in this dark eſtate,
    To ſee the good from ill,
And, binding nature faſt in fate,
    Left free the human will :—

4 What conſcience dictates to be done,
    Or warns me not to do,
This teach me more than hell to ſhun,
    That, more than heav'n purſue:

5 What bleſſings thy free bounty gives,
    Let me not caſt away;
For God is paid, when man receives;
    T' enjoy is to obey.

6 Yet not to earth's contracted span
　　Thy goodness let me bound,
　Or think thee Lord alone of man,
　　When thousand worlds are round.

7 Let not this weak, unknowing hand
　　Presume thy bolts to throw,
　And deal damnation round the land,
　　On each I judge thy foe.

8 If I am right, O teach my heart
　　Still in the right to stay;
　If I am wrong, thy grace impart,
　　To find the better way.

9 Save me alike from foolish pride,
　　Or impious discontent,
　At aught thy wisdom has deny'd,
　　Or aught thy goodness lent.

10 Teach me to feel another's wo,
　　To hide the fault I see;
　That mercy I to others show,
　　That mercy show to me.

11 Mean tho' I am, not wholly so,
　　Since quicken'd by thy breath;
　O lead me wheresoe'er I go,
　　Thro' this day's life or death.

12 This day, be bread and peace my lot;
　　All else beneath the sun
　Thou know'st if best bestow'd, or not—
　　And let thy will be done.

13 To THEE, whose temple is all space—
　　Whose altar, earth, sea, skies—
　One chorus let all being raise!
　　All nature's incense rise!

The SUBJECTS of the foregoing HYMNS, which are taken chiefly from the Salisbury Collection.

	Hymn
The divine Perfections	1— 8
Creation, Preservation, and temporal Blessings	9— 30
Blessings temporal and spiritual	31— 53
The Gospel Dispensation	54— 64
General Forms of Praise and Thanksgiving	65— 74
Adoration	75— 85
Confidence and Resignation	86—101
Faith, Holiness, and moral Virtues	102—128
Repentance and Pardon	129—132
Life, Death, and a future State	133—145
The Communion	146
Baptism	147—149
Ordination	150
At the Establishment of a religious Society	151
Funeral Hymn	152
Mission of Christ and the Spirit	153—156
New Year's Day	157—158
Publick Thanksgiving for national Blessings	159—162
Universal Prayer	163

A TABLE OF FIRST LINES.

A

	Hymn
ABBA, Father, God of love	151
Ah, wretched souls, who still remain	104
All-knowing God, 'tis thine to know	1
Almighty Author of our frame	65
Almighty Maker, God	9
And art thou with us, gracious Lord	87
Author of every work divine	154
Author of good, to thee we come	79
Awake our souls, away our fears	93
Awake my soul, lift up thine eyes	103
Awake my soul, stretch every nerve	105
Awake my soul, awake my tongue	51

B

Before Jehovah's awful throne	4
Before the awful throne we bow	66
Behold the morning sun	55
Behold the path which mortals tread	138
Behold the Lamb of God	146
Behold where breathing love divine	124
Be thou exalted, O my God	74
Beyond expression blest is he	129
Bless'd be the everlasting God	61
Blest are the humble souls who see	127
Blest be the grace which did proclaim	132

C

Can laughter feed th' immortal mind	116
Come weary souls with sin distrest	130
Come ye who love the Lord	143*
Commit thou all thy ways	97

                                                    Hymn
D
Death calls our friends, our neighbours hence   139

E
Eternal God, Almighty Cause   3
Eternal Source of life and thought   76
Eternal Source of every joy   13
Eternal Sovereign, Lord on high   162

F
Father of all, in every age   163
Father of all, thy care we bless   149
Father of everlasting love   155
Father of men, who can complain   60
Father of mercies, God of love   88
Fountain of being, God of love   85
Fountain of uncreated light   156
Frail is the state of mortal man   133
From all who dwell below the skies   74

G
Give to our God immortal praise   23
God of eternity, from thee   137
God of our life, thy constant care   157
God, who in various methods told   54
Great God, attend, while Sion sings   48
Great God, how endless is thy love   30
Great God, the heaven's well-order'd frame   10
Great God, this sacred day of thine   77
Great God, to thee our grateful tongues   28
Great God, to thee, the mighty King   6
Great God, we sing that mighty hand   158
Great Lord of earth, and seas, and skies   94
Great Ruler of the earth and skies   160

H
Had we the tongues of Greeks or Jews   125
Hail, the God of our salvation   57
Hail, thou eternal King   71
Happy is he who fears the Lord   121
Happy the souls who trust in God   91
Happy the soul whose early years   114

	Hymn
Hark from the tombs a doleful sound	46
He who hath made his refuge God	49
High in the heavens, eternal God	41
Holy, holy, holy Lord	70
How are thy servants bless'd, O Lord	29
How blest are they, how truly wise	150
How cheerful along the gay mead	19
How gentle God's commands	100
How greatly bless'd the man, whose ear	128
How happy is the Christian's state	109

I

If solid happiness we prize	117
I'll praise my Maker while I've breath	53
In all our Maker's vast designs	5
In the soft season of thy youth	115

J

Join every tongue to praise the Lord	12

L

Let every creature join	25
Let every mortal ear attend	64
Let every tongue thy goodness speak	52
Let party strife no more	122
Lift your voice, and thankful sing	22
Lo God is here! let us adore	75
Lo my Shepherd's hand divine	36
Lo what a feeble frame is ours	134
Lo what an entertaining sight	126
Long as we live we'll bless thy name	67
Lord, for the just thou dost provide	45
Lord, how mysterious are thy ways	95
Lord, thro' the dubious paths of life	81
Lord, we adore thy wond'rous name	90
Lord, what a feeble piece	135
Lord, what our ears have heard	147

	Hymn
Lord, when our raptur'd thought surveys	31
Loud be thy name ador'd	62

M

Mark the soft falling snow	59
Mistaken souls, who dream of heaven	102
My soul, abjure the accursed throng	120

N

Nor eye hath seen, nor ear hath heard	107
Now let our songs address the God of peace	159
Now let our souls on wings sublime	144

O

O come let us join	73
O come let us sing to the Lord a new song	161
O for an hymn of universal praise	26
O God, on thee we all depend	86
O God, our Father and our King	123
O happy souls who live on high	110
O Lord, how glorious is thy name	17
O praise the Lord, our heavenly King	43
O that the Lord would guide our ways	80
O thou the wretched's sure retreat	7
O thou who to our humble prayer	44
O 'tis a lovely thing to see	119
On thee, O God, we still depend	89
Our hearts shall triumph in the Lord	78
Our Maker and our King	69
Our Shepherd is the living Lord	33

P

Patience! O 'tis a grace divine	118
Praise God, from whom all blessings flow	63
Praise the Lord, let praise employ	27
Praise to God, immortal praise	15
Praise to the Sovereign of the sky	101
Praise to thy name, eternal God	84

Hymn

S

Shine on our souls, eternal God	83
Since thou, the everlasting God	92
Sing to the Lord a joyful song	50
So let our lips and lives express	106
Songs of immortal praise belong	20
Sovereign Lord of might and glory	72
Sovereign of life, before thine eye	140

T

The darken'd sky, how thick it lowers	98
The God of love will sure indulge	152
The heavens declare thy glory, Lord	56
The Lord is my shepherd, my guardian & guide	37
The Lord my pasture shall prepare	35
The Lord my shepherd is	34
The Lord of glory reigns, he reigns on high	8
The spacious firmament on high	2
The swift declining day	131
There is a God, all nature speaks	11
There is a land of pure delight	145
Thou God of our salvation	58
Thou Lord thro' every changing scene	148
Thy everlasting truth	141
Thy people Lord have ever found	96
Thy presence everlasting God	82
To-morrow Lord is thine	136

W

Wait on the Lord, ye heirs of hope	99
We bless the God, whose bounteous love	16
We bless the Lord, the great, the good	14
When all thy mercies, O my God	42
When Israel thro' the desert pass'd	32
When sickness shakes the languid frame	142
Wherewith shall I approach the Lord	112

Whoe'er with humble fear
Who shall to thy chosen seat

Y

Ye blest inhabitants of heaven
Ye humble souls, complain no more
Ye humble souls in God rejoice
Ye nations, round the earth rejoice
Ye sons of men, with joy record
Ye tribes of earth, in God rejoice

www.ingramcontent.com/pod-product-compliance
Lightning Source LLC
Chambersburg PA
CBHW022114160426
43197CB00009B/1012